Brothers of Orange

Jean and Denis Mesritz

By Monique Bond
with Jacki Ferro

Written by Monique Hélène Bond
with Jacki Ferro of Raw Memoirs www.rawmemoirs.com

ISBN: 978-1-922717-74-0 (paperback)
        978-1-922717-83-2 (eBook)

See also: https://fcbond.github.io/brothers-of-orange

National Library of Australia Cataloguing-In-Publication data is available at www.trove.nla.gov.au

A catalogue record for this book is available from the National Library of Australia

For Jean and Denis Mesritz.
Although you are no longer with us,
you are not forgotten.

The Song of the Eighteen Dead

A cell two metres long for me
But not two metres wide,
That plot of earth will smaller be
Whose whereabouts they hide;
But there unknown my rest I'll take,
My comrades with me slain;
Eighteen strong men saw morning break —
We'll see no dawn again.

Oh, bright and lovely land farewell!
Farewell free dunes and shore;
I vow that from the hour you fell,
I thought of ease no more;
What can a loyal man and true,
At such a time essay,
But bid his wife and child adieu
And fight the useless fray?

My task was hard, my duty stern
It brought me toil and strife,
But yet my heart would never turn
Back to my easy life.
Freedom was once in Netherlands
Both honoured and maintained,
Until the savage spoiler's hand
Its dwelling place profaned.

Until that lying boastful one
Lengthened his tale of shame,
When Netherlands was overrun
And we his serfs became.
Honour he claims, but knows it not
He glories in our grief,
And sorrows on our people brought
That false Germanic thief.

Berlin's Pied Piper pipes a tune
Seductive, false and sweet,
But sure as death is coming soon,
My love no more I'll greet,
Nor ever sup with her again,
Nor by her side will lie —
His seeming kindnesses disdain;
That fowler cruel and sly.

Remember always, you who read
These friends who with me die,
Kinsmen and all for whom we bleed
Keep green our memory,
As we have seen in days now gone
These words to you we say:
'The darkest night precedes the dawn,
All clouds must pass away.'

The early morning light I see
Gleams through that window high,
Dying, O God, a light make me,
My failures justify.
All men will err, though they may plan;
Thy mercy, Lord, I pray,
That I may quit the world a man
Before the squad today.

Jan Campert translated by E Prins and CM MacInnes.[1]

---

[1] *War Poetry from Occupied Holland*, Arrowsmith, 1945.

Note to readers

Key People Those whose stories are important to the overall tale of the Dutch resistance and the Mesritz family, but not necessarily to the lives of Jean and Denis, are included in a list of key people. Their names are set in bold italic type the first time they occur in any chapter.

References These have been divided into three sections: published works sorted by author; published works sorted by article or website title; and private letters and other unpublished works. We found this to be most convenient, and hope you will too.

Image credits Unless noted in the list at the end of the book, images are original photographs held or taken by members of the family.

Cover photos
Front: Jean Mesritz (left), at the time Kornet of the 2nd Regiment of Mounted Field Artillery of the Royal Netherlands Army. Master-in-Law Denis Mesritz (right), who published resistance journals and was a key leader of the 'Council of Nine', representing Dutch university students during World War II.

Back: The Verzetskruis (Dutch Cross of Resistance), as awarded to Denis Mesritz in May 1946: a bronze cross on a flaming star, surmounted by a crown, on which Saint George (the Resistance) kills the dragon (the Nazis). It is inscribed TROUW TOT IN DEN DOOD (loyal unto death).

Contents

Acknowledgements

Firstly, thanks to my brother, Luc Béliard, for sharing this journey to investigate the lives of our Dutch uncles. I would not have got very far if Luc had not come with me on my first fact-finding trip to Leiden and Groningen in 2013. Luc subsequently found many of the documents that shed light on our family's movements during the war. This book would not have been possible without his help and encouragement.

Thanks to Ron van Hasselt, author and researcher from Groningen, who transformed this project from 'too hard' to 'possible' by welcoming us to the Netherlands, introducing us to others who knew of Jean or Denis, and finding much valuable information, especially at the Netherlands Institute for War, Holocaust and Genocide Studies (NIOD). Thanks also to Colonel Michiel Teunisse for obtaining Jean's military records, and to Rien van Vliet, a supporter of war victims who shared his knowledge of the area and the history. Special thanks to dear friend Dini Elting who, for many years, helped us with Dutch documents, and to whom we owe enormous gratitude. Another special thanks to Tineke Schoonens for helping with research and translating so many documents.

I have enjoyed working on this as a family project with my three children, Denise, Francis and Helena, and my grandchildren, Kel, Claire and Arthur. They know how much it means to me. Special thanks to Denise for researching and writing the Background, to Francis for compiling the family tree, to Helena for coordinating copyediting and proofreading, and to all three grandchildren for accompanying me on trips to Europe and encouraging me with their interest.

Finally, thanks to writer and editor Jacki Ferro for working with me, my family, and our colleagues to bring the stories and research together, and to my friend, Megan Burrows, who became my de facto research assistant and shared so much of this journey with me. Without these helpers, I could not have created this book.

Preface

It is thanks to a very dear friend of mine, Margaret Marshall, that I wrote this book. In 2008, when Margaret was planning her visit to Europe, she told me that the first thing she wanted to see was the El Alamein Cemetery in northern Africa, where her uncle was buried. When Australia joined the war in 1940, Margaret's uncle, Bruce Weary, had immediately signed up and was soon involved with the Western Desert Campaign in Egypt and Libya, fighting in the Second Battle of El Alamein. He volunteered for what was a suicide mission. Private Weary of the Second Seventeenth gave his life for his comrades on the 29th of October 1942. Margaret really made me think: I knew about my father and our French family, but why was my mother's Dutch family such a mystery?

I knew that my mother had two brothers who had died during the war, and I was thinking about these two uncles when, by chance, someone told me of an interesting book, *Soldier of Orange*, by Dutch resistance fighter and WWII Royal Air Force (RAF) pilot **Erik Hazelhoff**. I was astonished to read that Erik spoke very highly of his friend, Jean Mesritz, who had also resisted the Nazi invasion of the Netherlands. This was one of my uncles! I wanted

Figure 1: When Margaret Marshall visited her uncle's grave at the El Alamein Commonwealth War Cemetery, she brought a photograph and bougainvillea flowers in his honour.

to know more about my mother's family, particularly these men. What roles had they played in the Dutch resistance?

By 2010, in Brisbane, Australia, our children were grown and making their own lives, while my husband Graham and I were interested in social justice, the environment and travel. I realised that more books were being written about World War II, and servicemen and women were sharing their experiences and the stories of their families and friends.

My brother Luc and I started gathering stories, both sad and inspiring, about our young Dutch uncles. In October 2013, I travelled to the Netherlands with Luc, his wife Aleth, and their friend Dini Elting, who kindly interpreted from Dutch for us all, to see some of the places where our uncles had lived.

Figure 2: (left to right) Monique Bond, Ron van Hasselt, Luc Béliard and Dini Elting on our first trip to Groningen, 2013.

The people we knew referred us to others, and so on, and thus we met Ron van Hasselt, a Holocaust researcher and author of six books (at last count) about people affected by the war. Thanks to Ron and his friends who were also willing to spend time with us in Groningen, we started to gain an understanding of Jean and Denis' lives. When we got home (France for Luc and Australia for me), we continued to research our mother's family.

The following is what we have been able to uncover about my Dutch uncles, Jean and Denis Mesritz.[2] We have drawn on diary entries from their father, Léo Mesritz (my maternal grandfather), family letters and photographs, and our memories of the little we knew from our mother about her family. We have also gathered historical information through the Netherlands Institute for War, Holocaust and Genocide Studies (NIOD),[3] books, and documents by associates of my uncles during those turbulent years of human suffering in Europe and indeed, the world.

---

[2] A pronunciation guide for English speakers: JEAN is pronounced with a soft J, like the G in 'massage'. The EA sounds like the AW in 'awning'. The final N is silent. DENIS, on the other hand is pronounced 'duh-knee'; the final S is silent. And MESRITZ is pronounced with two Z sounds: 'mez-ritz' (yes, the second syllable is like the hotel).

[3] The NIOD Institute is part of the Royal Netherlands Academy of Arts and Sciences, and its research and collections are open to those interested. NIOD's area of work covers the 20th and 21st centuries, with a focus on research into the effects of wars, the Holocaust and other genocides on individuals and society. See www.niod.nl/en.

Background

Our Australian family knows very little of our Dutch heritage, so this short introduction provides some context for the lives of our Dutch family.

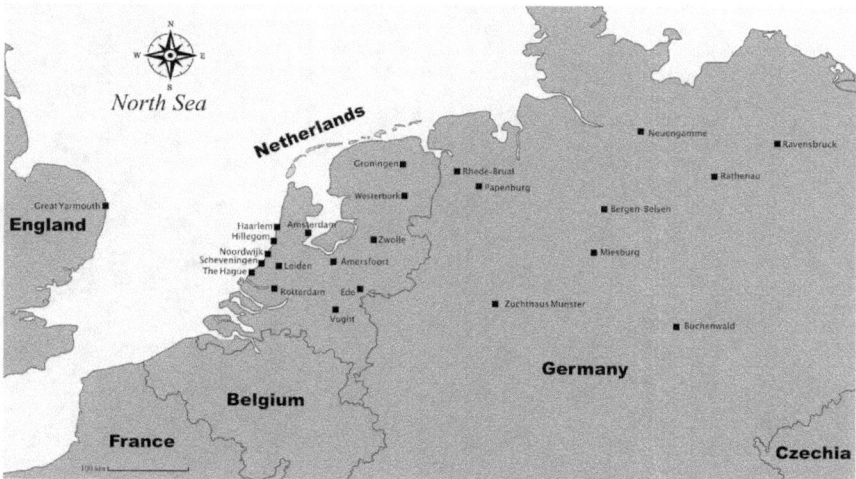

Figure 3: Map of the Nazi camps, and key places in the Netherlands, Germany and England referred to in this book.

The current Royal Kingdom of the Netherlands has twelve provinces, although at the time of World War II, there were only eleven, as Flevoland was not established until 1986. 'Holland' should only be used to refer to two of the eastern provinces,

North Holland and South Holland, but in practice is often used by English-speakers to refer to the whole of the Netherlands.[4]

Figure 4: Map of the Netherlands, noting the towns, rivers and places of interest referred to in this book.

---

[4] For more background information about the Netherlands see: www.holland. com/global/tourism.htm

Thanks to the quirks of our language, the inhabitants of the Netherlands are known in English as the Dutch. The Hague (Den Haag or 's-Gravenhage) is the administrative and royal capital, the seat of government, and the largest city on the Netherlands' Atlantic Coast. It is located in the province of South Holland, and also incorporates Scheveningen, originally a coastal village, which still has a long sandy beach and dunes. Amsterdam, in North Holland, is the largest city in the Netherlands, and its official capital.

A short way north-east of the Hague, the smaller town of Leiden has the oldest and most prestigious university of the Netherlands. About 240 kilometres from the Hague, north-east of both the Hague and Amsterdam, Groningen is another university town, an industrial centre, and the largest city in the northern Netherlands.

In the early part of the 20th century, many educated Dutch people spoke French at home, in preference to Dutch. So it was easy for Dutch people to live in France, and the French-speaking areas of Switzerland.

The Jewish Population of the Netherlands

Jewish people have been settling in what is now the Netherlands since the 1100s, and in greater numbers since the 1500s, after the country declared independence from the Catholic Spanish empire and embraced religious tolerance. By the 1800s, boundaries between Gentiles and Jews in the Netherlands were becoming less marked as there were more Gentile-Jewish marriages, and more residential integration and inclusion of Jewish people in civic and political institutions.

The Dutch census had a history of recording people's religion, and thus chronicled the number of people self-identifying as practising Judaism. The census of 1930 recorded 111,917 Jews living in the Netherlands, but in 1941 the Nazi occupation force considered 154,000 Dutch people to be Jewish.

Why such a large difference? In the Dutch census, identifying as Jewish was a matter of choice; however, under the Nazi administration, Jewishness was defined by descent. Anyone with one or more Jewish grandparents — specifically, a grandparent who was a member of the Jewish community — was considered a Jew.

The largest population of Dutch Jews lived in Amsterdam (about 80,000), with the next biggest population residing in the Hague. The vast majority of these identified as members of the Ashkenazi Dutch-Israelite community. In addition, about 2,500 Dutch people of Jewish descent were Christians — mostly Dutch Reformed, Calvinist Reformed or Catholic.

Timeline of WWII, focusing on Europe and the Netherlands

World War II Major Events	World War II in the Netherlands
18 Sep 1931 Imperial Japan invades Manchuria (north-eastern China).	
30 Jan 1933 The Nazi Party takes power and Hitler becomes Chancellor of Germany. **Oct 1935 – May 1936** Fascist Italy annexes Ethiopia. **25 Oct 1936** Nazi Germany and Fascist Italy sign the 'Rome–Berlin Axis Treaty'.	**1930s** The Netherlands is affected by the Great Depression, but in contrast to Germany concentrates on civil infrastructure programs to stimulate the economy, rather than military spending.
25 Nov 1936 Germany and Japan sign the 'Anti-Comintern Pact' against the Soviet Union and the international Communist movement.	
7 Jul 1937 Japan invades China.	
12 Mar 1938 Germany annexes Austria, making it part of Germany (the 'Anschluss').	
29 Sep 1938 Great Britain, France and Italy allow Germany to annex the 'Sudetenland' (the western, northern and southern border regions of Czechoslovakia) in exchange for a guarantee that Hitler will seek no further territorial gains. Hitler soon violates this agreement.	**1930s** The Netherlands maintains a neutral stance and trades freely with Germany (as do a number of other countries, including the United States), benefitting from the increased spending on military hardware.
9–10 Nov 1938 'Kristallnacht' (the 'night of broken glass'): in widespread pogroms in Germany, synagogues, and thousands of Jewish businesses, shops, homes, schools and cemeteries are destroyed. Around 30,000 Jewish men are arrested and taken to concentration camps. Over the next 10 months, 115,000 Jews emigrate from Germany.	

World War II Major Events	World War II in the Netherlands
1939	
Apr Italy invades Albania. **23 Aug** Germany and the Soviet Union sign a 'non-aggression agreement' and secretly divide Eastern Europe into 'spheres of influence'.	Military spending in the Netherlands doubles, but is still only 4% of national spending, compared with 25% in Germany.
1 Sep 1939 Germany invades Poland, marking the start of World War II in Europe.	
3 Sep France and Great Britain (and their colonies, including Australia) declare war on Germany. They, and others that join them, become known as the 'Allies'. **10 Sep** Canada declares war on Germany. **17 Sep** The Soviet Union invades Poland from the east in a bid to secure some Polish territory.	**Sep** The Netherlands declares its neutrality and remains neutral until May 1940. **Oct** The Dutch Government establishes Kamp Westerbork as a camp for Jewish refugees who have illegally entered the Netherlands (largely coming from Germany).
1940	
9 Apr Germany invades Denmark, which surrenders, and Norway, which holds out until 9 June, when it too surrenders.	
May–Jun In a series of lightning strikes ('Der Blitzkrieg'), Germany takes over much of western Europe. **10 Jun** Italy declares war on the Allies. The war extends into northern Africa. **14 Jun** The German army enters Paris.	**10 May** Nazi Germany invades the Netherlands. **13 May** The Dutch government and royal family flee to London to form a government in exile.

World War II Major Events	World War II in the Netherlands
22 Jun France surrenders and signs an armistice, allowing Germany to occupy the northern half and entire Channel and Atlantic coastlines of France. Southern France is ruled by a collaborationist regime, with its capital in the town of Vichy. A second armistice is signed with Italy on 24 June, and the two come into effect together on 25 June. **28 Jun** The Soviet Union forces Romania to cede two provinces. **Jun–Aug** The Soviet Union engineers communist 'coups d'état' to annex Baltic states as Soviet republics. **Jul–Oct** Germany attacks Great Britain by air in the 'Battle of Britain'.	**14 May** Germany bombs Rotterdam, targeting civilian areas. The Netherlands surrenders. **May** Austrian Nazi politician Arthur Seyss-Inquart is appointed Reichskommissar of the Occupied Netherlands. He initially takes a 'velvet glove' approach, and parts of the Dutch economy are stimulated by orders from Germany. But Seyss-Inquart soon starts removing Jews from positions in government, industry, the press, and academia. The German administration systematically eliminates non-Nazi organisations, flouting Dutch traditions of separate institutions, particularly for Catholics and Protestants. All socialist and communist parties are outlawed.
30 Aug Germany and Italy divide Transylvania between Romania and Hungary, triggering the rise of Antonescu's dictatorship of Romania. **13 Sep** Italy invades British-controlled Egypt. **27 Sep** Germany, Italy, and Japan sign the 'Tripartite Pact'; they and their allies become known as the 'Axis powers'. **Oct** Italy invades Greece. **Nov** Slovakia, Hungary, and Romania join the Axis powers.	**Oct** The 'Aryan Declaration' requires registration of all Jewish-owned businesses in the Netherlands; all Dutch civil servants, teachers, and scholars are told to sign.

World War II Major Events	World War II in the Netherlands
1941	
Feb Germany sends troops to reinforce Italy in northern Africa.	**10 Jan** Every Dutch resident must declare whether they have 'Jewish roots' (defined as anyone with at least one Jewish grandparent). Dutch Jews must have a large 'J' stamped on their identity papers. **22–23 Feb** At least 425 Dutch Jews are deported to concentration camps. In protest, the outlawed Dutch Communist Party joins with trade unions to organise a strike, which 300,000 people join, demanding the immediate release of the arrested Jews.
Mar Bulgaria joins the Axis powers.	**Mar** All parties, except the fascist National Socialist Movement, are forbidden in the Netherlands.
22 Jun The Axis powers attack the Soviet Union with a combined force of 4,000,000 troops. **7 Dec** Japan attacks the US Navy in Pearl Harbour, Hawaii. **8 Dec** The US joins Great Britain, Free France, and Poland as Allies against the Axis powers.	**Jun–Dec** Repression of Jews intensifies, and the first groups of Jews are deported to Mauthausen concentration camp in Austria. Living standards decline as Germany demands more contributions from the occupied territories.
7 Dec The Keitel Order, or 'Night and Fog Decree' pronounces that resistance fighters in occupied countries can be shot or transported to Germany without trial. These prisoners often vanish without a trace.	

World War II Major Events	World War II in the Netherlands
1942	
Apr Japan takes control of the Philippines, Indochina, and Singapore. **1942 – May 1945** British and US bombing reduces urban Germany to rubble.	**Mar** The 'Council of Nine' forms to co-ordinate resistance among Dutch universities. **3 May** Jews in the Netherlands are ordered to wear the Star of David badge (a six-pointed yellow star) on their clothing. **May** Construction of Kamp Vught begins, as a camp for Dutch political prisoners. It later becomes the only SS-controlled concentration camp.
4 Jun The US Navy defeats the Japanese Navy. **Jun–Sep** Axis armies attack the Soviet Union again. **Oct** The British win a decisive victory over Axis forces at El Alamein in Egypt.	**15 Jun** Deportation of Jews from the Netherlands to German-occupied Poland and Germany begins. Over the course of WWII, some 101,000 Jews are taken via Westerbork to extermination camps.
Nov US troops land in Morocco and Algeria, and soon combine with British and French forces to fight Rommel's German Africa Corps in Tunisia.	
Nov 1942 – Feb 1943 Soviet troops counterattack and surround the invading Axis troops. Hitler forbids the German sixth army from retreating or trying to break out of the Soviet ring, so survivors are forced to surrender.	

World War II Major Events	World War II in the Netherlands
1943	
13 May Axis forces in Tunisia surrender, ending the North African campaign.	
10 Jul The Allies invade Sicily.	
8 Sep Italy surrenders to the Allies, but Hitler helps Mussolini escape and set up government in northern Italy.	
1944	
6 Jun Allied forces land on the beaches of Normandy in the famous 'D-Day' campaign. They succeed in pushing back German forces.	**Autumn** Conditions in the Netherlands deteriorate further, leading to starvation and lack of fuel. Fanatical Nazis make a last stand and further destroy the country.
22 Jun The Soviet Union launches a massive offensive against Axis forces, from Belarus to Poland.	
Jul 1944 – Apr 1945 Soviet, US, and British forces liberate concentration camps throughout Europe, and discover the extent of the Nazi atrocities against inmates.	
25 Aug French and US forces liberate Paris from German control.	
12 Sep Finland leaves Axis, and ends the armistice with the Soviet Union.	**14 Sep** Allied forces reach Maastricht and liberate the city — the first in the Netherlands to be freed.
16 Dec Germany's final offensive, the 'Battle of the Bulge', attempts to re-conquer Belgium and split the Allied forces.	**Nov** Most of France, Belgium, and part of the southern Netherlands remain under German occupation and suffer famine throughout the 'Hunger Winter'.

World War II Major Events	World War II in the Netherlands
1945	
12 Jan A new Soviet offensive liberates Warsaw, Krakow, Budapest, and the rest of Hungary and Slovakia, and captures Vienna on 13 April 1945.	
22 Mar The US Army crosses the River Rhine into the German heartlands.	
16 Apr The Soviets encircle Berlin.	**16 Apr** Groningen is liberated.
Apr Tito leads Yugoslav partisan units to topple the pro-Nazi Ustasa regime in Croatia.	
7 May Germany surrenders to the Allies.	**5 May** The German Commander-in-Chief in the Netherlands surrenders to the Dutch Interior Forces. This date is now celebrated annually in the Netherlands as 'Liberation Day'.
8 May 1945 The Allies formally accept Germany's unconditional surrender: the war in Europe is over. This date is now celebrated annually in Europe as 'Victory in Europe Day', or 'VE Day'.	
6 Aug The US drops an atomic bomb on Hiroshima.	
8 Aug The Soviet Union declares war on Japan, and invades Manchuria (now north-eastern China).	
9 Aug The US drops an atomic bomb on Nagasaki.	
14 Aug Japan agrees, in principle, to surrender.	
2 Sep 1945 Japan surrenders to the US and Allies, and World War II ends.	

Key sources: *Holocaust Encyclopedia*, https://encyclopedia.ushmm.org, Anne Frank Museum, www.annefrank.org, English and Dutch Wikipedia.

Chapter 1

Searching for Answers

My mother, Marie Claire Alice Mesritz (Claire), did not want us to talk about our Dutch family — her family. She had married a cultured French army officer when she was very young, and soon her life in France with two small children seemed settled. But war was looming, and in November 1938 the chilling events of Kristallnacht[5] made it difficult to dismiss the increasing threats coming from Germany.

Germany invaded the Netherlands in May 1940, and things went from bad to worse. The Nazis were gaining power, and the first anti-Jewish regulations were issued almost immediately.

My father, Charles Paul Marie Béliard (Charles), served in the Army Supply Corps, as his injuries from gas attacks during the First World War kept him out of the front lines. By the autumn of 1940, Charles, now a Major, was posted to northern Africa.

---

[5] Also called the 'Night of Broken Glass', Kristallnacht occurred on the night of November 9–10 1938 when German Nazis attacked Jewish people and property throughout Germany. The name comes from the litter of broken glass left in the streets. More than 1,000 synagogues were burned, and rioters killed at least 91 Jews, ransacked about 7,500 Jewish businesses, and vandalised Jewish hospitals, homes, schools, and cemeteries. Some 30,000 Jewish men aged 16 to 60 were arrested.

The whole family — Charles, Claire and their two children, Marie Claire and Luc; Charles's mother, and his nephew Hubert Bartoli (at Hubert's request) — moved to Algeria, where they thought they would be safer than in France.

In 1941, my father suggested to Claire that they have another child, to be born as a symbol of hope. He believed that such a baby would be proof of the family's faith that they would survive and outlast the war. My mother agreed. So, on the 5th of July 1942, I was born in Constantine, Algeria. They named me Monique Hélène Béliard.

Figure 5: Claire Béliard (née Mesritz) and daughter Monique.

Growing up, I heard very little about my mother's brothers, except that two of them had died resisting the Nazi invasion of the Netherlands. Thinking back, it was understandable that the adults did not want to talk about the war. So much was unknown and unknowable, and the survivors wanted to look forward.

My maternal grandparents, Léo Mesritz and Ernestine Emma Claire Tiberghien, had four children — Claire, Lucien, Jean and Denis — born between 1915 and 1919. This book focuses on the lives of the two youngest sons.

My uncles were young men living in the Netherlands during World War II. Both held strong convictions against the Nazi regime, particularly its treatment of Jewish people. Jean was an attractive, gregarious, yet calm man. Despite being known as a 'gentle giant', Jean was a boxer, a member of the army reserve, and sought an actively combative role in the Royal Dutch Army. When war broke out he was also a scholar of law at Leiden University, the oldest and most prestigious university in the Netherlands. Denis, the youngest child, was awarded a Master of Law (LLM) from Groningen University during the war, even while working for the Dutch resistance. Denis took on key roles in coordinating the support of Dutch universities' academics and students, and in producing and disseminating the illegal newsletters that made up the resistance press, which were crucial to the Dutch resistance.

I knew none of these details until I started researching my uncles' lives.

In writing this account, we owe a great deal to *Jacob (Jos) de Vos*, a confidant and close friend of the Mesritz family. De Vos wrote long and thoughtful letters to several people who asked

Figure 6: In 1937, Jean enrolled in law at Leiden University.

after Jean or Denis. It is not always clear who the letters were written to; they started about two years after the war began and continued after the end of the war. These letters by De Vos give us the best idea of what Jean and Denis were like and of their actions during the war.

Erik Hazelhoff, a good friend of Jean's, also recorded details of Jean's character and his brave actions against the Nazi regime in his memoir *Soldier of Orange*, although some artistic license has been taken in the various versions now available in print, film, and as a musical.

On the 29th of April 1940, my grandfather Léo bought a diary. Thanks to its survival, we have a record of not only Léo's thoughts, discussions, actions and movements, but those of his family and friends too, as the war spread throughout the Netherlands and into France.

In early May 1940, Léo and Ernestine visited his mother, Madame Mulder, and their sons Jean and Denis in the Hague. By the time the Germans invaded the Netherlands on the 10th of May, Léo and Ernestine had returned to their home in Eze, in the south of France.

Both Léo and his brother Denis, who lived in Switzerland, quite often wrote to my parents, Claire (Léo's daughter) and Charles Béliard. Thus we have some information from France, Switzerland, and the Netherlands during the war. Many refugees from the Netherlands were going to France, and a great deal of thinking went into my grandfather Léo's plans. He discussed finances with his son-in-law Charles, and they both transferred money to England, which they hoped to recoup after the war.

My grandfather may have kept in contact with his sons, Jean and Denis, but sadly we have no record of this after he and his wife embarked on a boat for New York State in August 1940. At least Léo received word of his sons' welfare through letters from family and friends, such as their dear friend Jos de Vos. The final, dreadful confirmation of the boys' deaths came from the Red Cross.

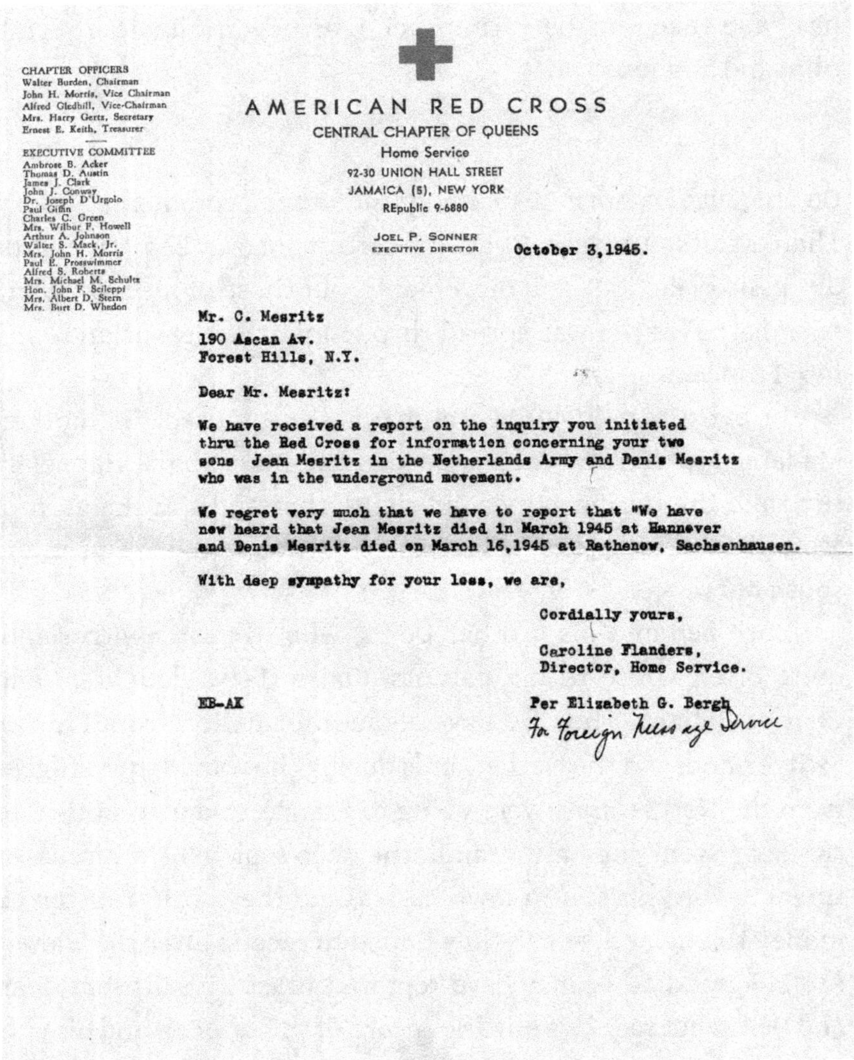

AMERICAN RED CROSS

CENTRAL CHAPTER OF QUEENS

Home Service

92-30 UNION HALL STREET

JAMAICA (5), NEW YORK

REpublic 9-6880

JOEL P. SONNER
EXECUTIVE DIRECTOR   October 3, 1945.

Mr. C. Mesritz
190 Ascan Av.
Forest Hills, N.Y.

Dear Mr. Mesritz:

We have received a report on the inquiry you initiated
thru the Red Cross for information concerning your two
sons   Jean Mesritz in the Netherlands Army and Denis Mesritz
who was in the underground movement.

We regret very much that we have to report that "We have
now heard that Jean Mesritz died in March 1945 at Hannover
and Denis Mesritz died on March 16, 1945 at Rathenov, Sachsenhausen.

With deep sympathy for your loss, we are,

Cordially yours,

Caroline Flanders,
Director, Home Service.

EB-AK

Per Elizabeth G. Bergh
For Foreign Message Service

Figure 7: This letter from the Red Cross confirms the deaths of both Jean and Denis.

Chapter 2

The Mesritz Family

My grandfather, Léo Mesritz, was from a Jewish family which had moved from the town of Mesritz (the German name for Międzyrzecz, which is now in Poland) to the Netherlands in 1812. Until 1892, immigrants did not have to become Dutch citizens but, from 1811, anyone who lived in the Netherlands was required to register a last name. As with many traditional societies, Ashkenazi Jews did not have a family surname that was passed down through the generations. They were given a first name, often followed by 'son of [their father's name]' or 'daughter of [their mother's name]'. To comply with Dutch requirements, Jews needed to change their Jewish name into a 'civil' last name. Families often adopted the name of the town they came from. Thus, Léo's great grandfather, Wolf Juda (Wolf, son of Juda) became Wolf Juda Mesritz (Wolf, 'son of Juda' from Mesritz).

Wolf Juda's son, Lion Wolf Mesritz, married Esther Bottenheim in 1836 and they had 11 children. Lion is buried in the Jewish cemetery at Almelo in the Netherlands.

One of their sons, August Mesritz (my great grandfather), renounced the Jewish religion to marry a Dutch Protestant, Maria Emelia Theresia Mulder ('Madame Mulder' hereafter), and they had three children: Therese, Léo and Denis. August became a colonial administrator in the Dutch Indies, and Léo, their middle child, was born in Semarang, in what is now Indonesia.

Figure 8: Madame Maria Emelia Theresia Mulder was a much-loved mother and grandmother. She provided a home in the Hague for grandsons Jean and Denis from 1929 until her death in 1943.

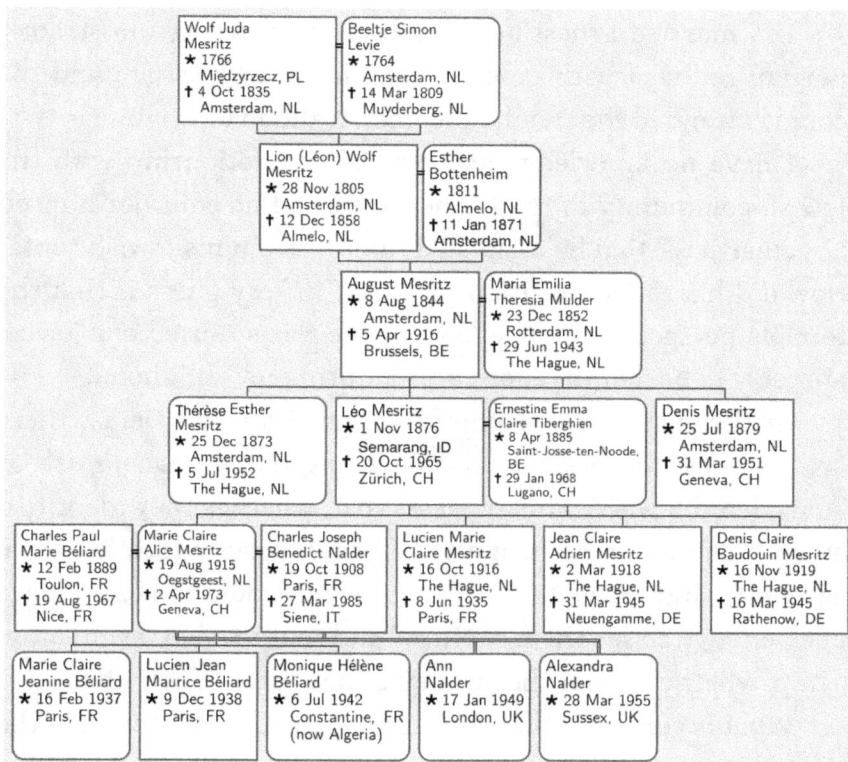

Figure 9: Extract from the Mesritz family tree.

Léo Mesritz was a Dutch lawyer and an enthusiastic scholar, who earned himself multiple doctorates — as far as we can tell, simply because he wanted to. Between 1914 and 1918, Léo worked as lead lawyer on the many mandatory agreements that allowed Shell Transport and Royal Dutch Petroleum to function as a single group, while maintaining separate entities quoted on different stock exchanges. He was able to set himself up with a generous income for life through astute negotiation of an ongoing percentage of oil revenues, rather than a high up-front fee for his services.

Léo married Ernestine Emma Claire Tiberghien (a striking Belgian redhead with green eyes). She was Christian, and the couple attended the Dutch Reformed Walloon Church.

I have no knowledge at all of Léo's relationship with the Jewish community in the Netherlands. Did he consider himself a secular Jew? Had he distanced himself from his Jewish roots? How did his active Protestant faith fit in? My guess is that the terrible persecution of the Jews by the Nazis caused our Jewish ancestry to become a taboo subject during my childhood.

In the historical documents about Jean and Denis, there are occasional references to their being Jewish, half-Jewish or 'considered Jewish'. This suggests that, whether they identified as such or not, some members of Dutch society labelled them as Jewish, and under Nazi occupation this could too easily have been enough to see them captured and sent to an extermination camp, whether or not they engaged in resistance activities.

What is certain is that the rate of persecution of Jews in the Netherlands was the highest in Western Europe during World War II: 75% of Dutch Jews were murdered. There is much to learn about how and why this happened, and the website of the Anne Frank Museum[6] is a good starting point. What is also certain is that a small number of brave people from many religions and walks of life resisted the Nazis, and Jean and Denis were part of this resistance from the very beginning of the occupation.

Whether Léo met the Nazi definition of 'Aryan' or 'non-Aryan' would have depended on whether the Nazis chose to

---

[6] The Anne Frank Museum has excellent online resources at: www.annefrank.org/en

define his grandfather, Lion Wolf Mesritz, as Jewish or not. The systematic and deadly persecution of Jews by the Nazis and their collaborators meant that this might have been a 'life or death' decision — maybe this was why my grandparents, Léo and Ernestine Mesritz, decided to leave Europe.

My Uncles' Generation

In about 1909, like many affluent Dutch families who had lived in the Dutch Indies, August Mesritz, Madame Mulder, and their three children returned to Holland and established themselves in the Hague.

Léo Mesritz married Ernestine Emma Claire Tiberghien and they had their first child, my mother. Marie Claire Alice Mesritz (Claire) was born at the Hague in the Netherlands on the 19th of August 1915. The first of my mother's younger brothers, Lucien,

Figure 10: Mesritz family portrait circa 1921. From left: Lucien, Jean, half-brother René Moreau (standing), mother Ernestine, Denis, and Claire.

was born in October 1916. The next, Jean Claire Adrien Mesritz, was born on the 2nd of March 1918. Léo and Ernestine's fourth and final child, Denis Claire Baudouin, was born on the 16th of November 1919. Throughout these years, the Mesritz family were members of the Dutch Reformed Walloon Church, and they resided in a prestigious neighbourhood, at Balistraat, 98, the Hague until 1929.

That year, Léo and Ernestine moved to Paris with their children, but chose separate places to live, in different parts of the city. We know that Claire, who was 14, cooked for Léo, and was also studying. Years later, she told me that she was unhappy with the situation, feeling it was unfair that she did not get enough time to study — she felt that, as a girl, her studies were not seen as very important. Yet Léo valued education highly, acquiring no fewer than five doctorates during his lifetime. Lucien, then aged 13, was also studying. Jean, aged 11, refused to stay in Paris and returned to live with his grandmother. Young Denis, aged nine, stayed in France for a while longer before returning to Holland. It seems both boys were happy to stay with Madame Mulder in the Hague.

Six years later, in June 1935, tragedy struck when Lucien died suddenly in Paris. He was only eighteen. Family stories suggest that he had appendicitis. In his final moments, Lucien asked his parents to hold each other's hands. He then asked them to promise that they would always live together. In the coming years, keeping this promise to their dying son would cause the family much grief.

Following Lucien's death, the Mesritz parents left Paris and moved to the enchanting village of Eze on the French Riviera.

Figure 11: Lucien, the oldest of the three Mesritz sons, pictured a short time before his death in June 1935. At eighteen, Lucien died suddenly in Paris, most likely from appendicitis.

They called their villa 'Omega', after the final letter in the Greek alphabet, to symbolise that this would be their last home together, where they would keep their promise to Lucien.

Just a few months before Lucien's death, on the 16th of February 1935, Claire married French army officer Charles Béliard. Charles was 26 years older than his young bride. He had signed up during WWI, on the 28th of July 1916, and served on the Front from July 1917–1919 as an Officer Cadet involved in military radio telegraphy.

Claire and Charles lived in Paris and, in February 1937, they welcomed their first child, Marie Claire. Their second child, a son named Lucien (known as Luc, and perhaps named after Claire's deceased older brother), was born in December 1938. Over the

Figure 12: Claire Mesritz married Charles Béliard, then a Major in the French army, on 16 February 1935 in southern France.

next couple of years, the young Béliard family often visited the Mesritz grandparents at their villa in Eze. Some summers, Dutch family and friends also joined them there.

In November 1938, Kristallnacht made it very clear that Jewish people were being targeted by the Nazis. Streams of Jewish families were leaving Germany and Austria, and 30,000 of them entered the Netherlands during the 1930s. Unfortunately, we have no record of what Léo, Ernestine, and their children were thinking as Hitler rose to power, and Europe was plunged into a second World War.

Family separations

In March 1939, Léo and Ernestine visited family and friends in Amsterdam and the Hague. Léo spent time with his sons, discussing their studies and the war.

Six months later, on the 3rd of September 1939, England and France declared war on Germany. Dutch people were concerned, but generally felt that the Germans would respect their neutrality, as they had in World War I. Army reserves — including the **Michielsen brothers** and Jean — were called up regularly for training.

In November 1939, my mother, Claire, offered her grandmother, Madame Mulder, a home in France. The family matriarch replied to Claire in a letter dated the 15th of November, thanking her for the offer, and explaining that she wanted to stay in her own country, the Netherlands, to maintain a home for her grandsons, Jean and Denis:

> *They know that here they are always received with open arms ... Jean is always so full of life when he comes on his two-day leave, and always leaves in the same mood when duty calls him.*

By January 1940, the Dutch and Belgian military had increased their level of alertness. On the 19th of April the Dutch declared 'martial law'. At the end of the month, my grandparents again visited Amsterdam. Léo wrote in his diary:

> *We dined in Amsterdam at the Padts. Milier is optimistic about the invasion. Mr Hoffelman explained to me at length, with the aid of a supporting diagram, that the German invasion could never succeed.*

On the 1st of May 1940, Léo spent time with Jean and Denis, who was down visiting from Groningen university. They discussed *the situation,* and Léo wrote that his sons *seemed optimistic* as they

Figure 13: Denis Mesritz (right) with his father, Léo.

talked about their studies and futures. The following day was Ascension Day. Although there was no service at the Walloon Church, Léo, Ernestine, and Denis attended a Dutch Reformed Church (the largest church body in the Netherlands at that time) in Hoefkade, where they heard *a beautiful sermon*. After lunch, they all visited Jean at his room in Leiden, where they also met Jean's dog. Events of *this gorgeous day* are recorded in Léo's diary:

The roads were packed with happy people, their cars and bicycles festooned with flowers.

Two days later, after attending a meeting in Haarlem, Léo travelled with colleagues by car to Amsterdam, a trip of some 30 kilometres. He recalled a serious talk about politics on the journey. Léo then drove south to his mother's house in the Hague to find Jean — dressed in a rabbit costume — on his way to a dance. Jean was always delighted to be invited to evening events, and he loved to dance.

On the following day, the 4th of May, Léo and Ernestine left the Netherlands, just as Dutch Prime Minister Dirk Jan de Geer began a speech against 'fifth columnists'.[7] A few days later, De Geer fled to London, from where he suggested that the Netherlands broker a separate peace with the Nazis. De Geer later wrote and published a controversial leaflet with 'instructions' for the people on how to cooperate with the Germans. His views so angered Queen Wilhelmina that she labelled him a *traitor and deserter to the Dutch cause*.[8]

Léo and Ernestine arrived back in Paris, where Claire was waiting for them at the Gare du Nord train station. The next

---

[7] A fifth column refers to any subversive group attempting to undermine a nation's solidarity, usually by supporting an enemy of the nation-state. By the late 1930s, as American involvement in WWII became more likely, 'fifth column' was commonly used to warn of potential disloyalty within the US. The fear of betrayal was heightened by the rapid fall of France in 1940, which some blamed on internal weakness and a pro-German 'fifth column'. www.britannica.com/topic/fifth-column, viewed 9 Dec 2020.

[8] After the war, former Dutch Prime Minister Dirk Jan de Geer was brought to trial, found guilty of high treason in time of war, stripped of all his honorary titles, and deprived of his title of Minister of State.

day, the family attended a church service in Passy, and shared dinner on the Champs-Elysées before travelling south to Claire and Charles's small country cottage in Thénisy. The following day, Léo took a walk with his granddaughter, Marie Claire. That afternoon, he received a letter from Jean asking if Léo wanted to sell his Peugeot 402.

On the evening of the 7th of May, disturbing news on the radio reported that all military leave from the Dutch army had been cancelled. A German invasion was imminent. On the 8th of May, Léo and Claire travelled north to Provins, from where he sent a telegram to Denis in Groningen, advising him to return to the Hague and sell the Peugeot.

Figure 14: Ernestine Tiberghien (left) and Léo Mesritz (right), my maternal grandparents.

After lunch the next day, Léo, with his wife and daughter, left Thénisy for Paris to meet up with Claire's husband, Major Charles

Béliard. Léo and Charles were both intellectuals and got along well. Over supper, Léo told Charles that, in Holland, they were counting on the motorised divisions that were waiting in the north of France. That night, Léo wrote in his diary: *I gathered he [Charles] wasn't particularly optimistic about this.* After dinner, Léo and Ernestine left Paris for Nice on the luxury train (operated by Wagon-Lits, who also ran the Orient Express).

In Berlin on the 9th of May, Dutch military embassy official Colonel Sas warned of an impending attack by the Nazis. But his alarm was ignored by superiors. At the station in Marseille, Léo bought a copy of *Le Petit Marseillais*. The paper maintained that the situation in Holland remained quite positive, and that people were relaxed.

However, when Léo and Ernestine arrived in Nice the following day, their worried daughter was there waiting. Claire told them that the Germans had invaded the Netherlands. The parents spent the night at their home in nearby Eze, and returned to Nice the next morning. Léo cabled New York to confirm his presence in Nice, and to the bank in the Hague, giving various instructions.

So, when Germany invaded the Netherlands on the 10th of May 1940, while the rest of the Mesritz family were in France, Jean and Denis remained in the Netherlands to continue their studies, and Jean, his military training. Each son, in his own way, then began working to free the Netherlands, and to resist the Nazi regime. No one could imagine then that they would each be captured and sent to concentration camps, and that both would die only months before the end of the war.

Seeking Refuge

We don't know exactly when Léo and Ernestine decided that they needed to leave France, but Léo's diary describes the uncertainty and growing desperation of people fleeing their homes as the Nazi army spread like a cancer across Europe. With Léo's Jewish heritage, it is possible that they decided to leave because they felt that Holland and occupied France would not be safe for them.

In Nice, on the 11th of May 1940, news on the radio remained favourable. Léo and Ernestine visited the Dutch consulate,

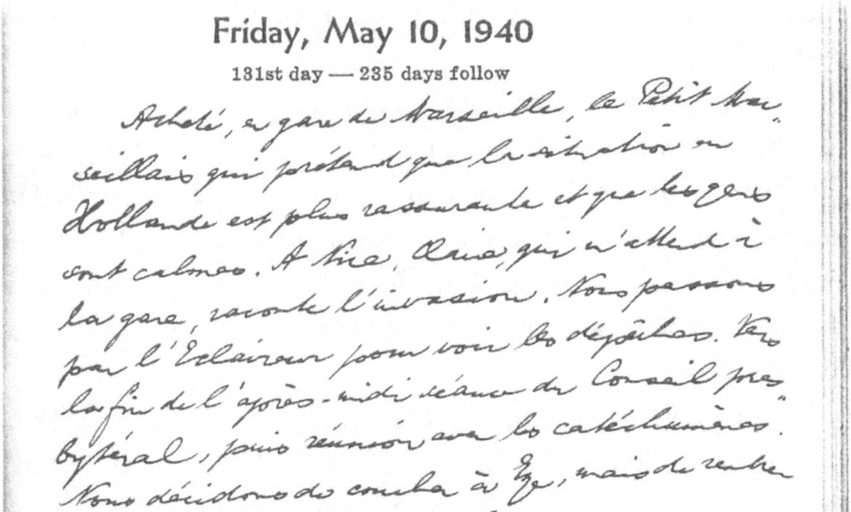

Friday, May 10, 1940

131st day — 235 days follow

Acheté, en gare de Marseille, le Petit Marseillais qui prétend que la situation en Hollande est plus rassurante et que les gens sont calmes. A Nice, Anna, qui m'attend à la gare, raconte l'invasion. Nous passons par l'Eclaireur pour voir les dépêches. Vers la fin de l'après-midi séance du Conseil presbytéral, puis réunion avec les catéchumènes. Nous décidons de coucher à Eze, mais de rentrer à Nice le lendemain matin.

Je télégraphie à New York, pour constater que je me trouve à Nice et à la banque à La Haye, pour donner diverses instructions.

Figure 15: A page of Léo's diary.

where they met with a Monsieur Van de Ree. Léo observed in his diary that everyone was *confident and optimistic*. That afternoon, they went looking to buy a wireless radio, as they needed to be able to hear the news. By the following day, however, Léo wrote that: *the news is not good*. He attended the Grand Whitsunday (or Pentecost) Service, which, he noted, was *a solemn procession*. A couple of days later, Léo received a cable from his son, Denis. It read: *Am in the Hague and all is well*. But all was not well, as Léo could no longer send cables back to the Hague, to his mother and sons.

On the 14th of May, Léo read in *L'Eclaireur* that the Dutch Army had surrendered. War-time rationing began at once. A couple of days later, with plenty of petrol available in southern France, even without coupons, Léo headed off to Eze. He wondered if the family should stay in Eze or move all the pictures, carpets, and silver to Nice for greater security. While in Eze, Léo received a call from Mademoiselle Marie Demètres,[9] advising Léo of worrying news about Italy from a friend, Lapinasse, at the censorship board. Marie and her family of several sisters were close friends of the Mesritz family, and they often helped one another. After this call, Léo decided to move their valuables to Nice.

Luxembourg fell to Germany, and there was fierce fighting in Belgium. In conversation, Léo noted that people remained optimistic, if a little disgusted by the poor resistance shown by the Netherlands. Over the next week, Léo continued to plan their

---

[9] The Demètres family remained close to the Mesritz and Béliard families. When I visited my father near Nice in 1956, as his home had no room for me, I stayed with the Demètres sisters.

move to Nice. He wrote: *Although the news is optimistic, no one feels reassured.* Léo further explained his unease:

> Lots of people in church. Madame Joëssel repeats to Ernestine about "our betrayal by Holland" ... Bad news from the north. Cable from Claire saying that she is in Toulouse with her children ... We go to Gréolliéres with Mademoiselle Marie ... We talk about the new decree that obliges foreign residents in France to deposit their American shares in French banks ... The above decree is withdrawn. First, a prayer meeting. A large crowd. We are still without news from the Netherlands.

On the 23rd of May, Léo received a letter from his daughter, Claire. She wanted to enrol in the Women's Auxiliary Service. On that day too, his son, Denis, sent Léo the small outstanding balance of funds held at the National Central Bank in Paris, plus 2,500 Swiss Francs. Léo continued to move the couple's possessions to Nice, attended Council meetings, and drove to Eze with Ernestine to collect a ration card for Claire. Léo had learned that Denis had joined the resistance, and he wrote to let him know that he disapproved, on the grounds that it *will be absolutely useless*, and that all he would achieve is that he *will be killed*. This is the only record we have of Léo's thoughts about Denis' work in the resistance.

A local parishioner suggested to Léo that the number of deaths in the Low Countries[10] had been grossly exaggerated.

---

[10] The Low Countries, or Lowlands, is a coastal region in north-western Europe — the lower basin of the Rhine–Meuse–Scheldt delta, consisting of Belgium, the Netherlands, and Luxembourg. Geographically and historically, the area also includes Flanders (France), East Frisia and Cleves (Germany). Over 18 days, around 6,000 Belgians were killed, 15,850 wounded and 200,000 captured as prisoners of war, according to Wikipedia.

On the 28th of May, however, Belgium capitulated as Nazi Germany invaded more of western Europe in a series of decisive strikes. Léo and Ernestine travelled to various French towns: they intended to visit their friends, the Van de Rees, but discovered that they had left for Marseilles. They then drove to Beaulieu to see Dr Ricoux, who gave Léo a travel document for Capvern (the French Pyrenees region), and the police station also provided a certificate of travel for Ernestine. In Eze, the couple asked their friends, the Bruns, to take care of their dog during their absence.

The 29th of May marked the last meeting of the season for the Eze Missions group where Léo attended church. He noted that the speaker, Pastor Lespinasse, who had been called up to service, arrived late. After the meeting, Léo wrote in his diary: *We have prayers, and Mademoiselle Monod prays for our sons.*

While continuing preparations to leave their home in Eze, Léo received word from a friend, Oscar Grovert, who was in the barracks at Marseille. Léo and Ernestine hoped to see Oscar on their way to Capvern. Léo's diary noted their final movements:

Ernestine's last sewing class ... We pack our suitcases and bags ... we go to Villa Philips and fill the car with 50 litres of petrol ... I talk with the commander and M. Boissy about events. M. Boissy is optimistic and says: "We'll get them." In the afternoon we go to the police station at Cap d'Ail with Mademoiselle Marie to collect the safe conduct for Ernestine ... we have tea at home in Eze and pay a visit to the Bruns ... The news seems to get worse and worse. Mr. Vandermerlen is the only man we have met who doesn't think that Italy will join the war ... We make a farewell visit to Villa Philips and load up our last barrels of petrol. The Demètres have also decided to leave.

After saying goodbye to friends, at 7 PM on the 4th of June 1940, Léo and Ernestine left their home in Eze for Le Trayas, wondering if they would ever see their friends again. Few people were on the roads, and Léo recorded that they were stopped many times to show their identity cards. Arriving at Marseille the next afternoon, the couple booked a hotel room. Their friend Oscar Grovert, and his twenty-three comrades, had all already left for England. At dinner, Léo and Ernestine had their identity cards checked by authorities yet again.

On the 6th of June, my grandparents left for Marignane and Born Lake in south-eastern France. Léo noted the large number of Belgians in the Hérault region as they drove further south, arriving at Carcassonne, just north of the Pyrenees. The next day, they travelled on to Toulouse. The roads were deserted, but the town was packed with refugees. The couple was greeted with good humour by their daughter Claire and her children, Marie Claire, now aged three, and Luc, aged eighteen months, who had travelled down from Thénisy, near Paris.

The following day, the family was on the move again. After a little shopping, in particular filling the cars with petrol, they were stopped to show their papers before arriving safely in Capvern, at the foot of the Pyrenees. On the 9th of June, Léo and Ernestine visited the mayor of Capvern to have their identity cards stamped, and then went to the police station nearby. Léo wrote:

More bad news on the radio. Newspapers are rare in Capvern.

On the 10th of June 1940, German forces closed in on the French capital. In Capvern, the weather turned cold and damp, and more refugees arrived. At news time, all the hotel guests gathered in the room where the wireless sat. Léo noted:

We usually turn up earlier than most so that we can hear the BBC. We learn from a Dutch transmission of a BBC broadcast at 18:00 hours that Italy has declared war on France and Great Britain.

Léo received a cable from his son-in-law Charles Béliard to say that he was delighted that Léo and the family had arrived safely in Capvern. But this day marked another sad turning point. Léo set up a radio in their hotel room and they heard that Paris was declared 'an open city'. Everyone realised that Paris would soon be taken.

On the 13th of June, Claire burst into her parents' room in tears. She had just heard French Prime Minister Paul Reynaud's speech: the first defeatist speech, in which Reynaud clearly stated that the only way the battle could continue would be for the Americans to join in, and no one believed that was likely. Léo noted in his diary that evening: *There is talk of total surrender.*

The next day, Léo, Ernestine, Claire and her children drove to Lourdes. Along the way, they discussed what to do if the Germans were to occupy France. They wrote to a young man named Guillaume, in Bordeaux, who planned to take a group to England. Léo also enquired if there were boats leaving for North Africa or the Dutch Antilles. On their return to Capvern, the group heard that the Germans had entered Paris on the previous night, the 13th of June.

The following day, Paris fell. Léo learnt more details of the occupation of Paris and the enemy advance: the Italians had just entered the war, and the Germans were threatening to invade the whole of France.

On the morning of the 16th of June, Léo received a telegram from his brother Denis in Geneva informing him that their mother, Madame Mulder, and Léo's sons, Jean and Denis, were all fine. This was the first news that Léo and the family had received from Holland since the occupation, a little over a month before. Léo, Ernestine and Claire thanked God for keeping their family safe. But the speed of the enemy's advance was becoming more concerning, so they decided to leave for Toulouse the following morning. Léo lovingly noted in his diary: *Little Claire packs my suitcase with her usual efficiency.*

News reached Léo that a new French Cabinet had been formed in Vichy, under the leadership of Marshal Pétain. The family travelled back to Toulouse, where they stayed with Madame Bartoli (Charles's sister) and her husband, Colonel Bartoli, of the French army. This must have been a very welcome offer, as Toulouse was in total chaos and bursting at the seams, with many people sleeping in their cars or on chairs in hotel lobbies. The Mesritz family were unable to extend Ernestine's passport in Toulouse, so on the morning of the 18th of June mother and daughter drove to Montauban seeking an extension of Ernestine's passport at the Dutch consulate. On their return, they had lunch with Madame Bartoli and her son Hubert. Léo noted that there was still plenty to eat, but a continuous flow of cars was arriving from Belgium and Paris. Léo and family investigated reaching Morocco by air, or even Martinique by sea, but no information was available. On the radio, they heard the newly appointed French Minister of the Interior, Charles Pomaret (appointed 16–26 June 1940), forbidding all foreigners from travelling.

On the 20th of June, cars were scattered everywhere, bursting with luggage. The family found a room at a hotel, and received news from Compiègne about the French Armistice. Authorities advised that it was unlikely the whole of France would be occupied, so the family decided to stay in Toulouse for a while. According to newspapers, negotiations with Italy had begun. Although the Italians had some thirty divisions available on their Alpine frontier, they had delayed their strike on south-eastern France until now, when the matter had been all-but settled. The attack, when it finally did come, made almost no progress against French defences.

The family in Toulouse managed to get their passports stamped to register their arrival in the town. When it was finally their turn, a Belgian employee wanted to send Léo away because the photo showed him wearing glasses. Fortunately, an employee from the Prefect's office came to sort it out, and all was settled. They also received another telegram from Denis in Switzerland to say that Madam Mulder and Léo's sons remained safe.

On the 22nd of June, the French Armistice with Germany was signed. *Thank goodness,* Léo wrote, *we find ourselves in the unoccupied part of the country.* But the armistice would not come into effect until an agreement was signed with Italy. The family installed the radio in their room and listened mostly to the BBC. At about 6 PM, Ernestine and Claire joined Léo in listening to the BBC transmission in Dutch, and then in French, which, Léo noted, *is not always easy.* Negotiations with Italy continued. Léo observed that food shops still appeared well stocked.

As they still had petrol, the family drove to the service at the Reformed church. They received a telegram from Mademoiselle

Marie saying that the Demètres family, who had been staying with Madame Deudon at Uzès, would return to Nice. Léo wrote: *Mr Churchill's attempts to keep France as an ally have failed.*

On the 24th of June, Charles Béliard visited his wife, young children, and parents-in-law in Toulouse, travelling about 50 kilometres from Montauban, where he was posted with the French General Headquarters. Charles was despondent: convinced that England would be invaded in the next few weeks. An armistice with Italy had now been signed, and the two treaties would come into force the following day. Claire decided to return to Montauban with Charles and spend a few days with him there.

The 25th of June 1940 was marked as a day of mourning. In Toulouse, a demonstration took place at the World War I memorial, 'Monument aux Combattants de la Haute-Garonne', and much anguish and sadness hung in the air. Claire, Charles, and their children left early for Montauban in their Peugeot 202. The Armistice came into force. Charles's mother, Madame Marie-Antoinette Béliard, shared with Léo that Charles had barely slept in the night, and that he was *very depressed*, which, Léo noted, *is not surprising.*

Two days later, Claire returned from Montauban, as Charles had been sent as part of the French delegation to the Italian Armistice. He had to leave in a great hurry by car to Bordeaux to take a plane to Italy. Léo observed that the papers no longer provided any serious news, and that French radio was useless. That left the BBC, but government authorities were beginning to suppress its broadcasts in French, and even in Dutch. The food shops were emptying. Léo managed to buy a few packets of biscuits and some Portuguese sardines, but there was no more cheese and, he noted, *not a hope of any butter for us.* That evening, when Léo went to the grocery store in the Rue de Metz, there were about seven or eight customers. One customer started railing against England, and everyone nodded in assent.

The last day that people could buy petrol, with or without coupons, was the 29th of June 1940. As the following day was Sunday, post offices would be closed. With their two cars, Léo and Claire went to Claire's vendor. He filled up the tanks and the cans they had with them. The family decided not to drive anymore, until the day they would be ready to leave. Ernestine was feeling unwell, so Léo went to church with his daughter, and word reached them that Charles was in Turin, northern Italy. By 2nd July, Ernestine was feeling better, so Léo went to the Dutch Vice Consulate with Claire. There they were told the devastating news that it would now be impossible for Dutch people to leave France and that, if they went to Spain, they would be sent to concentration camps.

Under Franco, neighbouring Spain had until now been neutral. However, with the fall of France, neutrality gave way to 'non-belligerence', and Franco had written to Hitler offering to join the war. Léo heard the rumour that Spain had declared war on England, and that ten German divisions had entered Spain.

Nonetheless, Léo was buoyed by his observation that correspondence with Nice and other towns in the unoccupied zone had become quite regular again. Letters and cards from Switzerland continued to arrive without serious delay, and Léo's brother Denis reconfirmed a number of times good news about Léo's mother and sons' welfare. On the other hand, travel by train had become terribly difficult, and Léo's letter of about ten days earlier to the Dutch Consular Official in Marseilles, Monsieur Van de Ree, had not yet received a reply.

On the 4th of July, Léo started investigating the possibility of going to Switzerland. They didn't want to go there, but reasoned that it would be safer than staying in France. Newspapers announced that the latest French Minister of the Interior (appointed 27 Jun – 6 Sep 1940), Monsieur Adrien Marquet, had taken measures *that will prevent foreigners from disturbing law and order.* Foreigners in France were still forbidden to travel, and anyone who did not conform to these measures was threatened with being interned.

Léo and Claire had to park their cars on the street, which they were unable to see from their hotel room. The next day, Léo, Ernestine and Claire all went to church on the tram. Most refugees, Léo observed, French as well as Belgians, just wanted to go home, but they were not allowed to. Belgians were not even allowed to leave the town where they had registered. Quite a number left anyway, without a 'safe-conduct permit'. Food shortages were becoming more serious but, as Léo wrote, *In the restaurants, the portions are always adequate.* According to Léo, 8th July was *a day like any other*, although shopping had become hard work. The daughter of Léo's brother Denis, Denise, was marrying a Swiss citizen, Monsieur Rappard. Claire and Léo tried to find something suitable as a wedding present for the newlyweds, and a small curio for Denise — there was still quite a choice to be had.

Charles asked Claire to move to Nice with their children for the time being, to be nearer to him in Turin. She was happy about this, of course, but delayed her departure, as her parents' plans were still so uncertain. The following day, the Mesritz family had a serious talk about where to go. Léo was not at all happy about the increasing restrictions on their freedom of travel, and he asked each of them to say what they thought. News from Charles in Turin about the status of the province of Nice was not optimistic. The family became ever more inclined to leave France.

On the 13th of July, a letter arrived from Geneva. Denis Mesritz had received Léo's telegram and letter requesting a Swiss visa. Léo's new nephew by marriage, Monsieur Rappard, was happy to help with the request. The Mesritz family was thrilled to hear this news, and appreciated the assistance of both Denis and Monsieur Rappard.

Léo and Ernestine's Escape

The family held long discussions about what they should do. Léo left it to his wife to decide between Nice, Switzerland, and America. Despite writing to a M. José Gari Gimero in Barcelona on the 24th of June, asking him to get them both visas for Spain, they had received no reply. The parents could, with help from their daughter and Madame Bartoli, ask the mayor of Toulouse for an introduction to the Spanish Consul, but what would be best to do? They agreed on one thing: they had to reach a final decision that week.

In Turin, Charles thought that his wife and children had already left for Nice. He had written to her there, which delayed his letters and, for reasons unknown, he hadn't received any letters from her. But Claire had remained in Toulouse, on account of her concern and affection for her parents. Claire thought that, when her parents finally left, she would be well placed to settle a number of things on their behalf. This increased the pressure on Léo and Ernestine to make up their minds about where to go.

On the 17th of July, the family received a 15-day visa for Switzerland. They decided, however, not to go there, but to instead try to get a letter of introduction to the Spanish Consul. Having no luck there, they resolved to try again the next day. Searching for medicine, Léo found that the shops were already out of stock. The 18th was a public holiday in Spain, so Léo was unable to try the Spanish Consul, but on the 19th, Léo and Ernestine visited the Spanish Consul and were granted visas. At dinner, they told Claire that they would go to Spain as soon as they got their French exit visas. They wanted to give Claire and Charles power of attorney, so that they could manage their affairs.

Léo and Ernestine went to the police station to get their exit visas stamped and, on the afternoon of the 21st of July, Léo wrote some letters. Among them was a letter to Monsieur Cuche, tendering Léo's resignation from the Presbyterian Council, as well as letters to Mademoiselle Marie Demètres, Denis Mesritz, Charles Béliard, Monsieur Brun, Madame Vernot, and Dr Pouy at Capvern. The couple began to prepare for their journey to Spain.

The next day, Léo discovered that the petrol had been stolen from their car and two tyres punctured. Claire offered to drive her parents to Perpignan, over 200 kilometres east of Toulouse. Nestled in the heart of the plain of Roussillon in southeast France, Perpignan lies a few kilometres from the Mediterranean Sea, and is the last major French city before Spain. The couple left everything from their car at Madame Bartoli's flat, where Colonel Bartoli agreed to look after their damaged car.

At 9 AM on the 24th of July, Claire picked up her parents. They filled Claire's car with their things and left Toulouse at 10 AM, but had to stop for a flat tyre, and again to show their papers. The following day, after Claire had driven them as far as she could, Léo and Ernestine bid a teary farewell to their daughter. All three of them were very emotional and Léo noted that his *poor little Claire has warm tears streaming down her face*. They could not know when or if they would see each other again.

Once they arrived in Barcelona, Léo and Ernestine spent a day going around the different travel agencies looking for options to travel by ship. The couple soon discovered that they were unable to exchange their French currency in Spain. On the 27th of July, they were issued visas for the Dutch Indies. They visited the British Consulate where they were told that, in Spain, only the Consulate in Madrid could arrange visas for South Africa, Canada, or the USA. The couple wrote several postcards to the Hague and to Nice. Back at the hotel, they packed their bags for Madrid. On the 28th of July, Léo and Ernestine left on the early train for Madrid, arriving by 11.15 AM. There they visited the US Consulate, where they were told they needed a letter of recommendation from the Dutch Consul. They left, and returned after getting the appropriate letter. Then they were told that they needed to provide evidence of the total funds in their bank account. So they went to the post office ...

With all requirements finally met, on the 30th of July 1940, Léo and Ernestine were granted visitor visas for the USA. In the following few days, they arranged their passage to New York. During their final days in Europe, the couple visited the Dutch Legation to say goodbye, and gave their forwarding address in

New York. With their exit visas granted, they sent a telegram to Claire in Nice, and their news to Léo's mother in the Hague and other relatives.

The parents packed their bags and, on the 2nd of August, travelled by train to Bilbao in northwest Spain, arriving at 8 PM. They spent the next day in Bilbao, unable to exchange Spanish currency.

Finally, at midnight on the 4th of August 1940, Léo and Ernestine Mesritz boarded the ship that would take them to safety in New York.

Chapter 3

Life Under Occupation

A full description of life in the Netherlands during World War II is beyond the scope of this book, but this brief overview of events provides context for Jean and Denis' resistance activities. Much more is available, from many different perspectives.

England and France had declared war on Germany on the 3rd of September 1939, but the general feeling among Dutch people at that time was that Germany would not declare war on the Netherlands — after all, they had not done so in World War I. Nonetheless, people were nervous, and Jean and his friends *Karel and Erik Michielsen,* who were all in the reserve army, were called up regularly for training.

Early on the morning of the 10th of May 1940, Germany invaded the Netherlands. The Nazis had not declared war, planning to catch the Dutch off-guard, and they succeeded in isolating the head of the Dutch army. The Germans wanted control of the airports and the city of the Hague, and they expected the Dutch to capitulate on the same day. According to *Erik Hazelhoff* in *Soldier of Orange,* Queen Wilhelmina, one of the few at the time who appreciated the extent of the Nazi threat, woke her daughter at 4 AM, saying simply, *They have come.*

Dutch airbases were attacked by Nazi air force bombers, airborne troops landed in the western part of the country, and Dutch lines were breached. Two members of the Dutch cabinet flew to London to solicit help, while Dutch police conducted mass arrests of Nazis and communists. French and English army units arrived in support of the Netherlands, and three days of fierce fighting followed.

Queen Wilhelmina and the royal family were in danger of capture by the Nazis. On Sunday the 12th of May, the Queen, accompanied by **François van 't Sant** and Crown Princess Juliana and her family, travelled to the Hook of Holland. At 11 PM, Princess Juliana and her family left the Netherlands aboard the British destroyer HMS *Codrington*. The following day, Cabinet advised Queen Wilhelmina to leave as well, which she did, aboard the HMS *Hereward* on the 13th of May. Although the Dutch Queen had retreated, and military resistance by her armed forces was not an option, she continued to reign, and the Dutch government to govern (to an extent) from British soil.

Like other members of the Dutch Royal House of Orange-Nassau, Major General François van 't Sant (Head Commissioner of Police, a leading intelligence figure, and a confidant of Queen Wilhelmina) had to leave his wife and daughter behind. In the exiled Dutch government in London, Van 't Sant served as Private Secretary to Queen Wilhelmina and Head of the Dutch central intelligence service, which was tasked with gathering information, supporting a domestic Dutch resistance, and committing sabotage in the German-occupied Netherlands.

His house in the Hague was confiscated by the 'Sicherheitsdienst'[11] and used as an office; its cellar was turned into a torture chamber.

On the 14th of May 1940, the German army bombed the city of Rotterdam, killing over a thousand civilians, destroying the homes of 85,000, and reducing the 'old' centre of Rotterdam to rubble. The Germans then threatened to do the same to other Dutch cities. Dutch General Henri Winkelman, aware of his army's limitations — 280,000 men were not enough to defend the entire country, and the Dutch army possessed no tanks and lacked sufficient field artillery and anti-aircraft guns — signed the Dutch capitulation, excluding Zeeland along the Belgian border where Dutch, Belgian and French troops continued to battle. The Netherlands had fallen, after only five days of fighting.

Following the capitulation of the Netherlands' armed forces, Hitler decided neither to take the Dutch army into captivity nor to apprehend them as prisoners of war, but to demobilise them. He demanded from the professional officers an 'Erewoord' (word of honour), in which the signatory promised not to take action against the interests of the German empire. There was confusion among the professional officers about whether or not to sign. Seventy-one Dutch army officers refused to sign and were taken to Germany as prisoners of war. Of those who did sign, many later joined illegal organisations in the resistance. Signing the 'Erewoord' counted heavily against these officers if they were arrested and convicted of resistance activities by the Nazis.

---

[11] The Sicherheitsdienst (SD) was the intelligence agency and police department of the SS and the Nazi Party in Nazi Germany and the occupied territories.

From the time of invasion, Dutch citizens came under the jurisdiction of the 'Wehrmacht' (the Nazi armed forces), but Wehrmacht control continued for less than a month. Soon a civil German government was formed and the Dutch parliament sent home. This differed greatly from the situation in Belgium, which remained under harsh German military rule.

The reason for the different treatment was that Hitler thought highly of the Dutch people, considering them fellow members of 'the Aryan master race'. Hitler's goal was to make the Netherlands part of Germany following the war. With this in mind, the transition to Nazi rule in the Netherlands was less abrupt and dramatic than in other European countries: the German administration initially adopted a 'velvet glove' approach. Nonetheless, *the German occupation killed more people in Holland than in any other country of Western Europe. One reason stood out: there was nowhere else for the people to go. Squeezed between Germany and the sea ... the way to England and freedom was blocked by ... the North Sea.*[12]

On the 29th of May 1940 in the Hague, newly-appointed Reichskommissar[13] Seyss-Inquart was installed as the highest German authority at a ceremony in the 'Ridderzaal' (Knights Hall) where, previously, Dutch kings and queens had given speeches at the start of parliamentary sessions. On the 2nd of July, General Winkelman, Commander-in-Chief of the Armed Forces of the Netherlands, was arrested and taken to Germany. Then refugees defined by the Nazis as 'non-Aryan' were ordered

---

[12] Erik Hazelhoff, *Soldier of Orange*, Hodder and Stoughton, 1972.
[13] The title of Reichskommissar was given by Adolf Hitler to a number of the Nazi governors of occupied countries during World War II.

to register. And on the 16th of September, the Nazi occupiers formed a Dutch SS unit from Dutch sympathisers.

The relatively uneventful transition had several effects. First, although the Dutch people were demoralised by their unexpected loss, they relaxed a bit. Many were deceived into believing that the Nazi occupation would entail neither great hardship nor atrocities. Dutch citizens had been shocked by Kristallnacht and the tales of atrocities against Jews in Vienna and other cities after Nazi invasion: of Jews forced to get down on their hands and knees to scrub the streets, synagogues burned to the ground, the rounding up of Jews into ghettos, and worse. But very few incidents of this nature happened during the initial implementation of German civil administration in the Netherlands. Second, Dutch culture and tradition reinforced the idea of obedience to the law. These two factors led many to believe that all they needed to do was outlast the German occupation. Many thought that the war would be short-lived and, thus, through a process of apparent cooperation and delay, the impact of Nazi occupation on the Dutch, including Dutch Jews, would be negligible.

But it was not long before things changed.

Impacts on Dutch Jews

The Nazi regime wasted little time in identifying and persecuting Dutch Jews. Just four months after the invasion of the Netherlands, on the 1st of October 1940, the Nazis pronounced the 'Aryan Declaration' (Ordinance 189/1940). This decreed that everyone aged fifteen years and older had to get a new identity card that stated their Jewish or non-Jewish status, according to rules specified by the Nazis. Jews were issued a special ID; non-Jews had to submit a Form A (Aryan). Under the Aryan Declaration, by the 26th of October, all civil servants, teachers and scholars had to sign a statement declaring their Jewish or non-Jewish status. Using these documents, German authorities compiled an inventory of who was Jewish and who was not.

The Aryan Declaration marked the start of a systematic and brutal regime of discrimination and maltreatment of Jewish people in the Netherlands. First the Dutch civil service was forbidden to hire or promote Jews, and then Dutch people with Jewish ancestors were dismissed from work. Travel became very difficult for those declared Jewish: in every street, police could ask for your identity papers; Jews were not allowed to use public transport; and the ID cards made it much harder for those trying to escape persecution to travel throughout Europe without getting caught.

While a minority of Dutch Jews went into hiding, the vast majority were sent to Nazi concentration camps. In January 1941, the first Dutch victims were sent to Mauthausen concentration camp, in Austria. By the end of the war, the Nazis, with assistance from local collaborators, had murdered 75% of Dutch Jews. During World War II, a total of 107,000 Jews were deported from the Netherlands. Of these, 102,000 perished in camps at the hands of the Nazis; only 5% survived. Some 30,000 Jews went into hiding. While two-thirds of these managed to survive, assisted by the Dutch underground,[14] the 10,000 who were discovered were deported and killed.

---

[14] This estimate is from the *Holocaust Encyclopedia*:
https://encyclopedia.ushmm.org/content/en/article/the-netherlands.

In addition, the property of many Dutch Jews and other Jewish people in the Netherlands was confiscated. It was not until the 1990s that the Dutch government made €181.5 million available to compensate the victims and their families.

In early 1941, Dutch theatres and cinemas were instructed to ban Jews, and the registration of all Jews began. By June of that year, public beaches and parks were off-limits to Jews, and on the 11th of June the Nazis conducted the second round-up of Amsterdam's Jews. By October, any Jews who worked required special permits, and Jewish university students in the Netherlands were banned from student associations. During the final two months of 1941, the Dutch registry of the textile industry withdrew the permits of 1,600 Jewish merchants, and all non-Dutch Jews were ordered to register for 'voluntary emigration'.

On the 7th of December 1941, the Keitel or 'Nacht und Nebel' (Night and Fog) Decree was issued. This decree meant that resistance fighters in occupied western European countries could be arrested, and either shot or sent away to concentration camps in Germany without trial. All contact with family and acquaintances was broken, and these prisoners disappeared, as it were, into the night and fog.

The Nazis formed the Nederlandse Kultuurkamer, an organisation tasked with 'Nazifying' arts and culture. All artists were required to become members if they wanted to exhibit, publish or perform. MC Escher, who had returned to the Netherlands from Italy, to escape Fascist rule there, was one of those who chose not to become a member. And it was during the war that his work turned from natural-inspired works to the transforming patterns for which he is now world-famous. Indeed, his 1938 work 'Day and Night' can readily be interpreted as two opposing visions of Europe's future.[15]

In early 1942, young Jewish men were sent to work camps within the Netherlands. By spring, all Jews were forced to wear a yellow star,[16] and Jewish patients at Dutch hospitals began to be deported. That summer, another large-scale round-up of Jews aged 15-40 took place in Amsterdam. Mass deportation of Jews from the Netherlands to Germany started in July.

On the 20th of April 1942, Dutch beaches were declared off-limits to civilians, and that summer the first large group of Dutch labour conscripts was transported to Germany. In the Hague and Rotterdam, the Nazis seized all bicycles.

By the spring of 1943, the Nazi grip on the Netherlands was tightening. Jews married to non-Jews were ordered to be sterilised, and Amsterdam's Jews were ordered to register at Kamp Westerbork for deportation. In autumn, in the final round-up of Jewish people in Amsterdam, another 10,000 people were captured and deported.

Dutch universities closed, and Jewish orphans were deported, mainly to camps in Poland. The Nazis lengthened the Dutch working week to 54 hours, and Dutch physicians went on

---

[15] For some examples of Escher's WWII works, and further discussion of their significance, see: gregcookland.com/wonderland/2018/02/01/m-c-escher

[16] Jews throughout Nazi-occupied Holland, Belgium, France, and Germany were forced to wear a yellow star (Star of David) as a means of identification. This was not a new idea; since medieval times, many European societies had forced their Jewish citizens to wear identifying badges. During WWII, in Poland, a white armband with a blue star marked Jewish people, while Greece, Croatia, Ukraine, Serbia, and Slovakia used other signs.

strike against the plan to 'Nazify' their profession. Rotterdam was bombed again — this time by the Allies, who were trying to destroy shipyards being used by the Germans — leaving still more Dutch civilians dead or homeless. All former Dutch soldiers were ordered into POW camps, and Dutch citizens were ordered to turn in all radios. By autumn 1943, the Germans had ordered a 72-hour working week. Life was getting very hard for the Dutch population.

Dutch Resistance

An early key player in the Dutch resistance was Jewish manual arts teacher, tapestry restorer, and carpet weaver, Bernardus IJzerdraat, who opposed fascism and communism as early as 1936. The day after the invasion of the Netherlands, IJzerdraat published the first edition of the *Geuzenbericht (Beggars' Message)*, a resistance pamphlet. On the 25th of November 1940, IJzerdraat was arrested in Haarlem. After a show trial, he was shot at Scheveningen prison on the 13th of March 1941, with fourteen other members of the resistance group 'De Geuzen' (The Beggars),[17] and three Amsterdam-based strikers. It is to

---

[17] On the 14th of May 1940, Bernardus IJzerdraat and others founded 'De Geuzen', the first Dutch resistance group of WWII. The original Geuzen were primarily Calvinist Dutch nobles who resisted Spanish rule in the sixteenth century, eventually leading to the establishment of an independent Dutch Republic. The rebels had initially been dismissed by a court councillor as only 'des gueux' or 'beggars', and the name was soon adopted by the patriots, who swore to remain "loyal to the King, even if it means carrying the beggar's pouch". Geuzen medals featuring this motto are valued Dutch historical artefacts.

these people that writer *Jan Campert* dedicated his famous poem, *De Achttien Doden* (*The Eighteen Dead*). Scheveningen prison was soon nicknamed the Oranjehotel (the Orange Hotel) by the Dutch, in tribute to the many resistance fighters imprisoned there. IJzerdraat was posthumously awarded the Dutch Cross of Resistance.

Another important leader of the Dutch resistance was banker and stockbroker *Walraven van Hall*. As war broke out, Van Hall established a fund to help families of merchant sailors who were stranded. He founded the Bank of Resistance and set up the Amsterdam Resistance Chapter with his brother Gijs (who later became mayor of Amsterdam). Van Hall was initially a member of the 'Nederlandse Unie' (Netherlands Union), formed in July 1940 to strengthen national identity and break through pre-war polarisation. While the Netherlands Union accepted the occupation of the Netherlands as a 'fait accompli' and therefore cooperated with the German occupiers, Van Hall actively opposed the Nazis. The Van Hall brothers, and a number of others, began financially supporting families who had been left without income because the breadwinner had been taken prisoner or worse.

In general, however, resistance in the Netherlands grew gradually, in response to escalating Nazi oppression. The occupiers were unprepared for the primarily non-militaristic character of the Dutch resistance. On the 10th of October 1940, after a show of resistance against the German presence in Noordoostpolder (a municipality in the central Netherlands), 130 Dutchmen were arrested and sent to the Buchenwald concentration camp in Germany.

Figure 16: Dutch banker and stockbroker Walraven van Hall founded the Bank of Resistance. In 1944, Van Hall became leader of the National Support Fund (NSF) that supported a variety of resistance groups and underground papers.

Following Himmler's order to round up Jews in Amsterdam in February 1941, the outlawed Dutch Communist Party joined with trade unions in protest, and organised a strike demanding 'the immediate release of the arrested Jews'. The strike spread quickly, with transport and dock workers also stopping work. The Germans retaliated with force, but the strike continued to spread and 300,000 people took part in what became known as 'the February strike' — one of the few large-scale protests made anywhere by non-Jews against Jewish persecution during WWII.

One of the most widespread resistance activities was hiding and sheltering refugees and enemies of the Nazi regime, which included concealing Jewish families, underground operatives, draft-age Dutchmen, and — later in the war — Allied aircrew. Collectively, these people in hiding were known as 'onderduikers' (under-divers).

The main organisation coordinating their support and protection was the Landelijke Organisatie Voor Hulp Aan Onderduikers (National Organisation for Help to People in Hiding), referred to as the 'LO'. Founder **Helena Kuipers-Rietberg** became increasingly involved as more and more Jews were rounded up and taken away. Helena was aided by the Reformed church Reverend Fritz Slomp, who was instrumental in encouraging people to offer refuge in their homes. The LO helped save thousands of people during WWII.

Around this time, Dutch businessman Jean Hendrik Weidner, who had fled from Paris after the German occupation of northern France in September 1939 to Lyon, in Vichy France, founded an escape network that would later become known as 'Dutch–Paris Resistance'. With its headquarters at Weidner's Lyonnaise textile business, the Dutch–Paris Resistance network comprised about 300 people and had ties to the Dutch, Belgian, and French resistance. Between 1942 and 1944, the Dutch–Paris Resistance rescued approximately 3,000 people from the Nazis — mostly Jews, resisters, labour draft evaders, and downed Allied aviators — and during the course of the war, they enabled about 1,000 people to reach Switzerland and Spain.

Dutch churches resisted the Nazis on another front. As had happened in Germany, the ranks of the clergy in the Netherlands were thinned through numerous arrests. Around 400 Roman

Catholics were arrested (49 of them never returned), the Netherlands Reformed Church lost 136 members (12 died in captivity), and the much smaller Reformed Churches lost 106 members (of whom 20 did not return). Many leaders in Dutch society at large shared a similar ordeal, but none were targeted like the Jewish community.

Many young people were forced to work against their will in the German war industry, and all Dutch men between the ages of 18 and 23 were required to participate in the Dutch Labour Service for six months.

Among the underground leaders of the domestic Dutch resistance were members of the **Boissevain family**. Jan 'Canada' Boissevain and his two eldest sons, Jan-Karel and Gideon, became involved in armed responses, particularly in the resistance group CS-6. Their mother, Mies Boissevain-van Lennep, and the third son, Frans, organised to hide, feed, and smuggle out many Jewish children and families. Jan-Karel and Gideon were shot by the Nazis, and Jan perished in a concentration camp; Mies and Frans barely survived a terrible year in concentration camps.[18]

Cornelia Willemina Boissevain, Jan's sister, married Denis Mesritz (Léo's brother). So Jean and Denis were linked by marriage to this family who worked so hard to resist the Nazis. Cornelia became a much-loved aunt and great aunt to the Mesritz family after the war. In 1945, 'Tante Tolly', as I knew her, showed

---

[18] John Tepper Marlin, 2015, *WW2 | 6. Armed Resistance: Jan Canada and Sons* (Updated 9 Feb 2016) https://cityeconomist.blogspot.com/2015/01/active-resistance-to-nazis-jan-canada.html

me great kindness when I was sent as a young child to regain my health in the Swiss mountains.

Resistance Press

Following German occupation on the 10th of May 1940, the Nazis quickly took control of the Dutch media. They enforced censorship and began producing Nazi propaganda. In response, independent Dutch citizens published their own uncensored, illegal papers. These papers were cherished by the population, and were better trusted than the official publications.

The **Drion brothers**, Jan and Huib, were writers and lawyers who found the compromising of freedom of expression under German occupation unbearable. The Drions chose to resist with words (rather than by sabotage, espionage or shooting). As early as August 1940, they started work on an illegal student magazine. Called *De Geus (The Beggar)* in reference to the original Geuzen rebels, the first issue appeared in October 1940; the final issue, No. 29, in 1945.

On the 10th of February 1941, the first issue of Dutch resistance paper *Het Parool* (the *Watchword*) was released. *Het Parool* became one of the most trusted Dutch newspapers by the end of the war and in the post-war period, when newspapers that had collaborated with the German occupier were banned from publication. *Het Parool* remains in publication today.

In 1944, financier Walraven van Hall became the leader of the National Support Fund (NSF). The fund supported resistance groups and papers, including *Het Parool* (the *Watchword*), *Vrij Nederland* (*Free Netherlands*), and *Trouw* (*Loyalty*) — a Protestant illegal paper. Publishing was always irregular, due to a lack of paper. In 1944, the Nazi occupiers tried to stop publication by rounding up and imprisoning some 23 couriers of *Trouw* and issuing an ultimatum; the editors did not give in. All 23 people captured were executed, just for handing out illegal papers.

De Kern (*The Core*) was established in February 1944, when contact meetings began among representatives of various resistance organisations, such as the Ordedienst (OD), the Landelijke Knokploegen (LKP) (also known as 'the thugs'), the National Committee of Resistance (NC), the National Support Fund (NSF), the Raad van Verzet (RVV, Council of Resistance), the Identity Card Centre (PBC),[19] and the Protestant *Trouw* group. *De Kern*'s goal was to improve mutual cooperation.

University Resistance

In June 1940, **Benjamin Marius Telders**, Professor of International Law at Leiden University and Chair of the Liberal State Party, published a series of four articles in the *Nieuwe Rotterdamsche Courant* (*New Rotterdam Courier*). From the outset, Telders drew a clear line — he was willing to cooperate with and obey the German occupiers, provided that they complied with all international rules and norms, and allowed the Dutch people the freedom to preserve their own beliefs and traditions. In his articles, Telders detailed how the Dutch should behave under the new circumstances and where the boundaries of the German powers lay. If the occupying power exceeded these limits,

---

[19] Forged identity cards were vital to every aspect of resistance work. The Persoonsbewijzencentrale (PBC), or Identity Card Centre, produced around 80,000 counterfeit identity cards during WWII. www.tracesofwar.com/ articles/5329/Raid-on-the-Population-Registry-of-Amsterdam.htm

Telders argued, civil servants, for example, would have the right to refuse to cooperate.[20]

In September 1940, Professor Telders, Professor P Scholten, and the politician and journalist Dr Herman Bernard Wiardi Beckman published the brochure *Den Vaderland Ghetrouwe* (*Faithful to the Fatherland*), a collection of three defiant lectures. Telders emphasised that the Netherlands wanted to remain a country of democracy, freedom and justice. This publication appeared legally and gained wide circulation, much to the annoyance of the German administration.

In November, Professor Telders organised a protest after having heard that Jewish staff at Leiden University would be fired, including their highly esteemed colleague, Professor Eduard Maurits Meijers.[21] At 10 AM on the 26th of November, fellow lecturer in law **Professor Rudolf Pabus Cleveringa** delivered an inspirational address, in which he protested against the German occupation's orders to dismiss Jewish colleagues.[22] That afternoon, Cleveringa was arrested and taken to the Oranjehotel. The professor had anticipated this, and came to work with a bag already packed according to Hazelhoff, in *Soldier of Orange*.

---

[20] CM Schulten. *Zeg mij aan wien ik toebehoor [Tell me to whom I belong]*. Rijksinstituut voor Oorlogsdocumentatie, 1993, p. 137. Translated from Dutch by Tineke Schoonens.

[21] Professor Eduard Maurits Meijers was sent to camps throughout the war but survived. After the war, he was asked by royal order to design a new civil code for the Netherlands.

[22] View Professor Cleveringa's 'Protest Address' at www.universiteitleiden. nl/binaries/content/assets/algemeen/oraties/cleveringa-oratie/teksten/ protest-speech-rudolph-cleveringa.pdf.

Students at Delft College and Leiden University held a 48-hour strike in support of their Jewish professors — the first in a series of strikes against such decrees. Leiden students also typed out Cleveringa's lecture and, led by a student named André Koch, circulated it to universities throughout Holland. Leiden University and Delft College were subsequently closed down indefinitely by German forces.

In December 1940, Professor Telders was also arrested and taken to the Oranjehotel.

Figure 17: Professors Telders (left) and Cleveringa (right) who worked together to protest anti-Jewish policies at Leiden University. Denis worked with Telders in the student resistance, and Jean was incarcerated with both professors in the Oranjehotel (Scheveningen prison).

In March 1942, Denis Mesritz of Groningen University, and other academics, formed the 'Council of Nine' to co-ordinate the resistance among Dutch universities. The Council became a consultative body for students of higher education, and maintained contact at the inter-academic level across the Netherlands. Comprising representatives from the nine cities where Dutch universities or technical colleges were located, the council represented 15,000 students. Denis and **Gustaaf Henri (Han) Gelder** were foremen, coordinating resistance activities. The Council maintained contact with two Dutch resistance groups, the LO and the Identity Card Centre (PBC), and produced and distributed many illegal resistance papers.

Armed Resistance

On the 28th of August 1944, the Landelijke Knokploegen (LKP) — the National Assault Group of the LO and the 'crack team' of the Dutch resistance — received its first large arms drop. A decree from the Dutch government in exile, in London, merged all resistance groups into one, unified fighting force under central command. As Allied troops — the 'Prinses Irene Brigade'[23] (Royal Dutch Brigade) among them — inched their way toward Dutch soil, the Dutch resistance movement formed itself into an underground army. At the start it was ill-equipped and poorly trained, but this army matured quickly in its ongoing battle with an enemy that had never observed any international conventions

---

[23] The Prinses Irene Brigade was a Dutch army unit established in 1941, and decommissioned in 1945, after the end of WWII. It consisted of Dutch troops outside the Netherlands, and volunteers from many countries, including Dutch emigrants and their children. The brigade was based in England and Canada, and was involved in action during the liberation of France, Belgium and the Netherlands.

of war. If caught, resistance fighters faced certain death. In spite of all this, vacancies caused by arrests were filled quickly, even when the Germans intensified their oppression.

Food Rationing and the Hunger Winter

On the 14th of September 1940, just four months after the German invasion, meat rationing began in the Netherlands. By April 1941, milk and potatoes were also rationed. By June, natural gas and electricity were rationed.

The Nazi occupation lasted five years, with devastating consequences for all Dutch people, culminating in the 'Hunger Winter' (Nov 1944 to Apr 1945). In September 1944, a Dutch railway strike was called, to try to disrupt German troop movements. The Germans retaliated with a blockade of food and coal supplies to the Netherlands, and people starved.

In late December 1944, Germany ordered men aged 16 to 40 years old to report for labour conscription. In a two-day roundup for forced labour in Rotterdam and Schiedam, the Germans captured 50,000 men, and these large-scale manhunts further terrorised the population. Amsterdam closed its famous city park, Vondelpark, to visitors after people in starving households cut down most of its trees for fuel. Hunger drove many — including the elderly, women and children — on long treks in search of food, often with no success.

Between 18,000 and 22,000 people died during the Hunger Winter, mostly in the cities. Children were sent to the countryside, people burnt their furniture to keep warm, and some had nothing to eat but sugar beets and tulip bulbs (with the poisonous centres removed). By February 1945, adults were limited to 580 calories a day, and even the black market was empty of food.[24]

---

[24] 'The Hunger Winter: The Dutch famine of 1944–45' by Ailish Lalor, *Dutch Review*, 19 February, 2021.

Chapter 4

Jean's Resolve

When Léo and Ernestine moved to Paris in 1929 with Lucien and Claire, their two younger sons (eleven-year-old Jean and nine-year-old Denis) remained in Holland with their grandmother, Madame Mulder. Maybe the boys stayed to keep their grandmother company, maybe to complete their Dutch education — we don't know for sure. Madame Mulder's comfortable home was located in a prestigious neighbourhood, at Cornelis Houtmanstraat 56, the Hague, only a few blocks from the beautiful 'Haagse bos' (the Hague Forest) and the 'Huis ten Bosch', one of three royal palaces.

Figure 18: Léo's mother, Madame Maria Mesritz-Mulder, proudly escorted by grandson Jean Mesritz.

On his first day of middle school, in about 1926, young Jean Mesritz shared a bench seat with **Erik Hazelhoff**. It was the start of a close friendship. In his memoir, *Soldier of Orange*, Erik recalls that Jean was much admired and looked up to by their school friends. Describing Jean as a handsome, well-built fellow, Erik recalled how the pair had gone on to high school together and maintained their friendship afterwards. Girls often fell for Jean — for his intelligence, light eyes and fine complexion — and he was Erik's mentor on such matters; he knew how to get on with women and make them feel safe.

Jean was a robust, outgoing young man. For a while, the two young men took boxing lessons together, yet among his university friends, Jean was known as a calm and gentle giant. Serious enough about defending his country to have enlisted in the Royal Netherlands Army Reserve in 1937, at the same time, Jean enrolled in law at the prestigious Leiden University.

The Mesritz and Hazelhoff families were among many Dutch families from the East Indies who returned to Holland in the years before World War II. Léo Mesritz had been born in Semarang, Indonesia. In the next generation, Erik Hazelhoff was born in Surabaya, Java; and **Karel and Erik Michielsen** in Padang, Sumatra. These families mainly lived in the same neighbourhood in the Hague, were affluent, and knew each other well. Throughout the 1930s, the 'Den Haag' youngsters formed a close community.

The group included the Mesritz brothers, Erik Hazelhoff, **Lodo van Hamel** (also known as Ludo), and brothers Karel and Erik Michielsen. Karel got to know them a little later, having lived in Batavia in the East Indies from 1932–37. Jean was especially close to Erik Hazelhoff, while Lodo was closer to Jean's older

Figure 19: The 'Den Haag' children grew up messing about in boats. Here two of the Mesritz boys take the oars.

brother, Lucien. Denis, being younger, was less involved with that group of friends.

In September 1937, Jean and his friends Erik Hazelhoff and Karel Michielsen, among others, enrolled at Leiden University. As Hazelhoff noted, *The idea of going through life without a degree did not appeal to any of us.* Leiden was 'the university' for lawyers, and Jean's father, Léo, had attended Leiden many years earlier. You could specialise in international law, maritime law, or family law, but it was said that lazy students studied general law, as it looked good on your resumé when going for a job.

All of the boys had plenty of free time to enjoy student life and joined the Leiden University student association, the Minerva Club. Formed in 1814, the Minerva prides itself on being the oldest student association of the Netherlands.

In the same month as enrolling at university, nineteen-year-old Jean enlisted in the 2nd Regiment of the Mounted Field Artillery of the Royal Netherlands Army. He particularly loved working with the horses. From the 13th of September he was a normal soldier from the municipality of the Hague, with Army Registration No. 18.03.02.016, under number 1755. By early December, Jean was appointed to the Officers School at Ede with the rank of Corporal, and by the following March he was promoted to Sergeant Titular. Six months later, Jean was promoted again to Sergeant, before being sent home for leave on the 2nd of September 1938.

Jean's resistance to the Nazi regime ran deep. On the 10th of November 1938 — the night after Kristallnacht — Jean climbed on top of a table at the Minerva Club and asked everyone present to think about what was happening with Hitler and the Jews. In his memoir, Hazelhoff records that he was quite surprised, and always maintained his belief that he had never before that night realised that Jean was Jewish: *Jean Mesritz, Jewish? It had simply never come up. And why should it? What difference did it make?* After Jean's actions, some Minerva members thought him out of line, bringing the Jewish matter up uninvited.

Karel Michielsen later described Jean as *a policy-minded, but uncompromising student heavyweight champion. He loved Paris and Scheveningen, but infinitely more without Krauts, whom he held in intense contempt.*[25]

The Mesritz family had not been practising Jews for three generations, and it is impossible for me to know if they still felt

---

[25] Karel Michielsen. *Bygone Glory.* Unpublished memoirs, courtesy of Karel Michielsen junior, 2013.

themselves part of the Jewish community. It does seem, from the records, that some people considered Jean to be Jewish. In the Netherlands in 1938, being Jewish did not have any grave implications, but this would soon change.

In January 1939, Jean was promoted to Kornet as a junior Probationary Officer (the equivalent of a junior Commissioned Officer in the British system). Following further training, he returned home again for leave in June.

Invasion

The Nazis began planning their invasion of Poland. Great Britain guaranteed that they would come to the assistance of Poland if Germany attacked. In May 1939, the Dutch government admitted to harbouring 8,000 German refugees. By the 26th of August, Jean was called back to the army for war mobilisation. Erik Michielsen was also drafted into military service, after four years of study. The Dutch government had started to realise that Germany might invade the Netherlands.

On the 1st of September 1939, the German battleship *Schleswig-Holstein* opened bombardment on the Westerplatte, a Polish military base, firing what were, according to many sources, the first shots of World War II. Three days later, the Dutch government issued a 'Declaration of Neutrality'. On the 3rd of September, England and France declared war on Germany. The Dutch assumed that they would remain neutral, as they had during World War I. Some even say that, initially, the Dutch government were unsure whether they would need to defend their country against England or Germany.

By October, the Dutch government had established a camp at Westerbork in the north-eastern Netherlands to intern Jewish refugees who had entered the country 'illegally'. Meanwhile, at Leiden University, most Minerva members remained unconcerned about a possible conflict. Later that month, the Dutch government ordered the Royal Army to prepare for war. On the 10th of December 1939, Jean was granted special leave from the army to study.

When Nazi Germany invaded the Netherlands on the 10th of May 1940, Kornet Jean Mesritz was serving in the Royal Netherlands Army. During the Battle of the Grebbeberg, which began the following day, of the Leiden University set, only Erik Michielsen saw action. Throughout May, Michielsen manned command posts at various bridges and at Valkenburg airfield, before being demobilised at the end of the month.

In the Hague, Erik Hazelhoff and Karel Michielsen were growing increasingly angry. Many high-ranking and well-to-do Dutch leaders had fled to England, and were sitting there being paid great wages, yet apparently doing nothing to help the Dutch people as the invaders advanced. Jean's friends wanted to work for the Dutch government in exile and actively fight the Nazis.

But some parts of the Dutch government were active. In London on the 27th of August 1940, their 'Den Haag' friend, Lodo van Hamel, now a Dutch naval officer, was commissioned by the Dutch government in exile as a spy. Van Hamel had escaped the Netherlands during its initial invasion, reaching England by trawler on the evening of the 14th of May. From there, he had been active in the evacuation of British troops from Dunkirk as commander of motorboat 74, which he sailed provocatively under a Dutch flag.

Major General François Van 't Sant asked Van Hamel to return to the Netherlands as their first secret agent, to prepare the ground for a Dutch intelligence service. Lodo was responsible for establishing a reliable radio connection to London, and setting up an espionage group.

Attempts to Cross to England

On the 29th of May 1940, Karel Michelsen celebrated his birthday by beginning to plan an escape from the occupied Netherlands. Granted leave from the army, Karel planned to go to England, where he could fight the Nazi forces more effectively. Jean was still in active service, so Karel did not include him.

The plan hinged around *Kees van Eendenburg* (which translates as 'Duckburg'), a friend a little older than Karel, who owned a 12 foot dinghy, the *Bebek* ('Duck' in Indonesian). It was simple but daring: three men would row across to England in the *Bebek*.

In *Soldier of Orange*, Erik Hazelhoff recalls how outlandish he thought the idea was:

> Firstly, to outwit the Germans and set sail was impossible, but then to cross the murderous North Sea in a little, open, twelve-foot hull? ... the way to England and freedom was blocked by more than a hundred miles of statistically the most deadly body of water in the world, the North Sea.

Later, when the terror and counter-terror of occupation and resistance convulsed the Netherlands, Britain looked like a haven; but from 1940 to 1942, the opposite was true. As Hazelhoff noted, *He who crossed over must sacrifice all he loved, including his life, to fight the Nazis.*

Figure 20: Brothers Karel (left) and Erik (right) Michielsen. Karel was one of the first Dutch resistance fighters to successfully traverse the treacherous North Sea, inspiring many other Dutchmen. Erik and Jean Mesritz both tried to reach England in 1940; Erik finally made it in June 1942, and joined the Air Force.

By horse and carriage, Van Eendenburg, Karel Michielsen, and **Fred Vas Nunes** took the *Bebek* from its inland mooring at the Kaag around 20 kilometres away, to the beach near Oegstgeest where Van Eendenburg lived. They stored food, water, and life jackets with friends who lived on the promenade. The Germans watched as the group practised regularly for weeks to get through the surf, dressed only in swimming trunks.

After the bombing of Rotterdam on the 14th of May, most of the Dutch Army surrendered (although not the Navy, nor those forces fighting in Zeeland on the Belgian border). Thus, on the 14th of June, Jean Mesritz was demobilised and sent home to the

Hague for 'great leave'. As a Reserve Officer, to his regret, Jean was forced into unemployment because the Royal Netherlands Army no longer existed. This was a challenge, as he then had no income. Like his friend Karel, Jean sought an opportunity to travel to England to participate actively in the war from there, but the timing just didn't work for him to join Karel and his friends in their escape attempt. Although his chances of success were minimal, Jean wanted to get out of the Netherlands, both because he wanted to learn to fight in planes against the Nazis, and because of his perceived Jewish surname. Jean, with his Leiden friends, took the plunge into defiance.

Soon word came that no more vessels would be allowed on Dutch beaches. Although the weather was poor, the young trio of resistors — Kees van Eendenburg, Karel Michielsen and Fred vas Nunes — could postpone their escape no longer. On the 5th of July, they left Holland for Great Yarmouth (see Figure 3).[26] When the Germans asked them what they were doing, they explained that, due to the incoming ban, they would be taking the boat to Scheveningen, some 10 kilometres to the south, and so they were allowed to leave. By the time the Germans noticed that the group was not headed towards Scheveningen, but towards the open sea, the *Bebek* was out of range of the Nazi rifles.

In the Netherlands at the time, only a small proportion of Leideners were trying to reach England. Some felt they needed to finish their studies first, while others thought it too dangerous.

---

[26] When the three men arrived in England, they were received by Queen Wilhelmina at Roehampton Park. Without consulting the government, the Queen awarded each the Bronze Cross.

Figure 21: Jean Mesritz, the 'gentle giant', was outgoing and had many friends. Girls were attracted to him, and he knew how to get on with them and make them feel safe.

Still others, like Erik Hazelhoff, were plotting and planning, but finding life very confusing. And when summer's warmth faded, the crossing would become still more risky, with storms and cold North Sea waters as dangerous as Nazi obstruction.

Jean Mesritz and his cohort developed aliases: Jean became 'Bruno', *Carel Kranenburg* was known as 'the Hussar', Herman van Brero[27] was 'Count B', and Erik Michielsen was simply 'Erik'. As Hazelhoff recounts in *Soldier of Orange*:

A long-awaited meeting with a man named 'Bruno' produced my oldest friend from school, Jean Mesritz, a Jewish fellow Leidener of great charm and brilliance.

On the 7th of July, Karel Michielsen, Van Eendenburg and Vas Nunes drew near their destination, Great Yarmouth, and were intercepted by the British minesweeper, HMS *Grampian*. Three Leiden men had successfully crossed from the Netherlands to Great Britain! In the minds of those in the Dutch resistance, their

---

[27] Herman van Brero escaped the Netherlands in November 1940 by a roundabout route, signing on with Chris Krediet as cooks on coastal steamers as far as Finland, then crossing the world, to finally reach the United States.

safe crossing shattered Holland's isolation — the Nazi prison had cracked. Their success provided an enormous boost to others planning their own crossings, but it also resulted in the Germans tightening their security.

Karel Michielsen was soon called to the exiled Dutch government offices of Van 't Sant, who was playing a key role in combined Dutch–British intelligence operations. During their meeting, Van 't Sant asked Karel to provide a list of those he considered trustworthy, and who would be prepared to give their lives in the Allied cause. Karel suggested three people: his older brother Erik Michielsen, Jan ten Bosch (**Iman Jacob Pieter van den Bosch**), and Jean Mesritz.

Finally, I finished my list of people whom I believed to be totally trustworthy for the Allied cause and who'd sacrifice their life therefore, with the name Jean Mesritz. I served with Jean in Ede. He was a Jew, fiercely anti-German, hated NSB members [a Dutch fascist political party] and Nazis and was a champion heavy weight amateur boxer. I hadn't included him in our Katwijk overwhelming plan as he was still mobilised in the service in the East of the country and I hadn't been able to get hold of him during the two days when I was looking for seven people. A few weeks later when we were preparing our escape with Bebek I was in regular contact with him. I knew that he was literally not scared of anything.

One afternoon when the two of us were walking across the Rapenburg in Leiden reminiscing about our war experiences, two girls and a Jew were being bothered by a trio of somewhat drunk German soldiers. Jean immediately flew up at them and, with his imposing figure and even more threatening attitude, the Krauts retreated hastily with their tails between their legs. I considered that very courageous behaviour from a man who was obviously of Jewish descent and could still impose himself on three armed Jew-haters. Consequently, I also included the address and telephone number of Jean and with that finished my first list.[28]

In the Netherlands, the Nazis were becoming more of a threat. Many of Jean Mesritz's friends began to take notice. They started training for war, and quite a few decided that the most effective approach would be to get to England as soon as possible. There they could train for the Air Force or Navy, and return to fight the Nazis.

Jean was deep in conversation with his mentor **Jos de Vos**, a close friend of the family, about how best to fight for freedom for his compatriots. In a letter to Jean and Denis' parents (my grandparents Léo and Ernestine Mesritz) dated the 25th of June 1945, De Vos wrote:

As you know, Jean was demobilised in June 1940. The Germans had not sent the Dutch army into captivity ... in the hope of disposing the Dutch in their favour but they did not succeed. Jean, as a reserve officer, was then forced into unemployment, to his great regret, and was apparently seeking an opportunity to go to England to participate actively in the war there. The chance to go was minimal. In August 1940, during one of his visits to my office, I had a very serious conversation with

---

[28] Michielsen, Karel. *Bygone Glory*. Unpublished memoirs, courtesy of Karel Michielsen Junior, 2013.

him on this subject and I urged him to be very careful. Our conversation ended with his words:

"Right now, there is little chance for me to go to England. So, be quiet. But if I find a good opportunity, then I will know what I should do. My parents and my grandmother will understand my approach."

Shortly after this conversation, Jean, Anton de Haseth Möller (Anton Muller), Erik Michielsen, and Carel Kranenburg bought two canoes. They painted the canoes a dark, inconspicuous colour and fastened them together with sturdy crossbars, then mounted an outboard motor on the right side. For rations, they collected four Edam cheeses and 80 bars of chocolate. On the 13th of August 1940, they thought themselves ready to go, but then Erik Michielsen ran into Erik Hazelhoff.

Hazelhoff proposed a different plan. The group made a deal with Van der Zwan, the skipper of the SCH 107 fishing boat: they would stowaway on board. Though the fishing fleet was under constant surveillance by German warships, the skipper would signal the stowaways when he reached the outer limits of the area where he was allowed to fish, and they would launch the lifeboat, fitted with an outboard motor for the occasion so the stowaways could motor to within reach of the British. They would give the skipper 500 guilders as compensation, so that he could buy a new boat.

Everything was brought onboard but, just before leaving, they were warned by Jean's friend Chris Krediet[29] and the skipper

---

[29] A friend of Jean Mesritz, Chris Krediet successfully reached England in 1941 via the US, and worked on 'Contact Holland' with Erik Hazelhoff to establish reliable radio contact throughout the war.

Figure 22: Jean Mesritz and Carel Kranenburg in Leiden in August 1940, during a test paddle for their planned escape to England. They bound two canoes together to give more stability for crossing the North Sea.

that two German soldiers would go with them as guards. The skipper backed out of the deal and the plan fell through.

The following day, the 14th of August, the same group planned to sneak onto a trawler and steal a lifeboat. They bought an outboard engine and provisions, and Jean and another of the men took service pistols. Again, their plans were foiled by Nazis boarding the boat.

Undeterred, the very next day, the four men decided to cross in the canoes. But the tiny boats were very risky for the long crossing, and could only fit four. Hazelhoff had an outboard motor and some petrol, so he persuaded them to spend yet more money and effort on a larger boat, which would fit all five of them, and offer a better chance of success in the weather conditions. They bought a heavy lapstrake dinghy at De Kaag, and all met up on the sea dunes at Noordwijk, about 12 kilometres out of Leiden. As they launched the dinghy, Erik Michielsen and Anton took the oars, while Carel, Jean and Erik Hazelhoff sat.

Unfortunately, the winds were very strong, and the sea and surf choppy. Both Jean and Hazelhoff became seriously seasick, and the boat began to take on water. On reaching open sea, they attempted to hook on the motor, but a lateral wave upset the boat. Although they managed to right it, the vessel was taking on too much water. They jettisoned the engine, but the boat sank anyway. The group endured a total of five-and-a-half hours, both in and out of the water, before reaching the beach from which they had departed. Their dinghy crossing had failed, and they all returned to Leiden.

On the 19th of August, Erik Hazelhoff decided to go alone, using a rowboat owned by the Scheveningen Beach Club, which the lifeguards used to float around among the swimmers. Erik had got hold of a small outboard motor and some illegal petrol, but the lids of the petrol cans were not well-secured; when he arrived at night to launch the boat, the petrol had gone from the bathing shed where the cans were hidden. It turned out that in the heat, the lids had popped off, and the smell of petrol gave away its location. Erik's friend Gijs, who was not aware of the plan to cross that night, had taken it home for safekeeping. So Erik could not go, and they were all very discouraged.

Meanwhile, with the cooperation of the Dutch section of MI6 (the UK Secret Service), on the 28th of August, Dutch naval officer Lodo van Hamel became the first secret agent dropped into the occupied Netherlands. The RAF parachuted Van Hamel into a bulb field at Hillegom. He brought with him a transmitter to set up reliable communications between the Dutch government in the UK and the local resistance. In his first couple of weeks, Lodo was in almost daily contact with London via the transmitter.

On the 2nd of September, Jean, Erik Michielsen, Carel Kranenburg, and Anton Muller tried once more to take their two canoes across the North Sea, again from Noordwijk. Luckily, they ran into Van Brero, who warned them of a new German machine gun post right on their path. Due to this, and the approaching autumn storms, no further crossing attempts to England could be made in 1940.

A couple of weeks later, while walking down a street in the Hague, Jean recognised Lodo van Hamel, who was using the alias Willem van Dalen. Van Hamel had been a friend of Jean's older brother Lucien, since they had attended the Lyceum[30] together.

Jean immediately guessed the truth about Van Hamel's undercover role, and urged Van Hamel to take him back to England with him. Lodo agreed, but only after certain other people were brought into the group. Through Lodo, Jean and his friends heard various details about the situation in England.

---

[30] A lyceum is a type of selective secondary school in the Netherlands and other European countries.

Van Hamel knew little more than the others about the recently launched German aerial bombardments and the Battle of Britain,[31] but a few media reports impressed on the group just how dangerous it was to hold views against the Nazis.

By late September, Van Hamel had completed his task and was ready to return to London to continue his work for the Dutch intelligence service there. His forged passport was of poor quality, however, and the risk of arrest was great if it was given more than a cursory inspection.

Jean's friend, Leiden medical student **Hans Hers** was working for MI6 with Van Hamel, and helping to organise the all-important return to England. They planned for Van Hamel, joined by Jean Mesritz, **Marion Smit**, and **Professor Lourens Baas Becking**, to be picked up by a seaplane at the Frisian Tjeukemeer (Lake Tjeuke), which lies about 160 kilometres north of Leiden. In preparation, Hans Hers, Erik Michielsen, **Wim Eggink**, and others went to Lake Tjeuke, and discovered an excellent landing area for the seaplane.

In a statement on 16th October 1945, Hans Hers recalled how the group had reached Heerenveen, near Lake Tjeuke, the day before the planned escape:

> *I departed at 8 o'clock in the morning by train to Friesland to prepare the bare necessities. Van Hamel escorted me to the Staatsspoor station in the Hague and he gave me his suitcase*

---

[31] The Battle of Britain (10 July – 31 October 1940) was the first large-scale military campaign fought by air forces only. Both the Royal Air Force (RAF) and the Royal Navy's Fleet Air Arm (FAA) defended the UK against the Luftwaffe, Hitler's air force. The Battle of Britain overlaps 'the Blitz', which featured night attacks on cities from 7 September 1940 to 11 May 1941.

with material he had been gathering together. J.C.A. [Jean]
Mesritz travelled with me to Zwolle. From there, he went to
Groningen from where he could go to Heerenveen, close to the
Tjeukemeer. The others, including Van Hamel, were to meet
in Heerenveen on October 13. The place to meet was the hotel-
restaurant Verminnen, opposite the station.[32]

Jean's Arrest

On the night of the 13th of October 1940, secret agent Van Hamel
and his friends were on high alert. They were out on Lake Tjeuke
in a small boat, awaiting a Fokker seaplane (T.VIII/W of the
320nd Dutch Squadron RAF) that was carrying out a dangerous
flight into occupied Dutch territory to fetch them. The plane
would take them to England to join the Dutch army there. The
group were disguised as ornithologists, and their cover story
was that they had come to study bird migration. A suitcase
containing espionage material was already hidden on one of
the small islands in the lake. They waited the whole night for
nothing; pilot Heije Schaper, officer-observer Ritte and corporal
Van Tongeren could not land because of ground fog — the plane
flew over, but left.

On the 14th of October 1940, the group again waited at
Lake Tjeuke. Once more, the Fokker was unable to land due
to low hanging fog. Pilot Schaper made a series of ever-lower
landing passes over more than fifteen minutes, but the visibility
was simply too poor. He had to abort the mission and return to
England.

---

[32] JFPh Hers. 'Statement made on October 15, 1945'. Courtesy of NIOD.

But the night-time roar over the lake had been noticed. On the morning of 15th October, two Dutch policemen from the National Guard appeared and arrested everyone. They tried to persuade the police officers to let them go, but one officer had already informed his pro-German superior of the arrest, and the Nazis had been alerted. The five captured conspirators were handed over to the SS, transferred to the House of Custody in Leeuwarden, and taken from there to the Oranjehotel prison in Scheveningen.

Talking with good friend and fellow resistance fighter Erik Hazelhoff, Erik Michielsen described the arrest:

They got Jean. Also got Ludo van Hamel, who was shot a year later by Germans. Ludo never gave a single name. They dressed

Figure 23: Lodo van Hamel, the first Dutch secret agent dropped into the occupied Netherlands. A childhood friend of the Mesritz family, Van Hamel was arrested at Lake Tjeuke with Jean, and executed by the Germans at the Bussumerheide (near Kamp Crailo) on 16 June 1941.

Figure 24: RAF fighter pilot Erik Hazelhoff was involved in numerous undercover missions for the exiled Dutch government during WWII. Close childhood friends, Jean and Erik both attempted to reach England in 1940.

up as birdwatchers, but a farmer's wife saw them, thought they planned to steal her eel (caught in nets) and alarmed the police, who told the Germans. After the first attempt failed (fog), they were arrested. Pilot Heye Schaper (awarded Militaire Willems-Orde) came back the next day and was shot at. He managed to escape.[33]

On the night of the 15th of October, visibility was good, so Schaper tried again to land on Lake Tjeuke, unaware that the group had already been arrested. The agreed light signal was observed — at least the observer and the telegrapher recognised it as such. Schaper landed cautiously and taxied his plane towards a small boat in the middle of the lake. When the boat was at a distance of

---

[33] Erik Hazelhoff. *Soldier of Orange.* Hodder and Stoughton, 1972.

about 50 metres, however, searchlights suddenly flashed on and the aircraft came under fire from all sides. Clearly, something had gone very wrong. As Corporal Van Tongeren returned fire, Schaper accelerated, taking off in a risky zigzag. Quickly reaching a safe altitude, Schaper set course for Felixstowe.

It was a narrow escape: two crew members were injured, and the Fokker, which had been shot at by a machine gun and German defence rifles, was badly damaged. It was not until after they landed that the crew realised the aircraft had been hit approximately forty times. They had killed ten of the German soldiers who ambushed them.

Afterwards, the exiled Dutch army learned that their potential passengers had been arrested and handed over to the Germans. Unfortunately, the hidden suitcase was also found by police and handed over to 'the moffen'.[34] Now all of Van Hamel's activities were known. In the papers, the Germans found the name Allers: the Allers family were subsequently arrested and, in their home, the Germans found some coded messages.

Van Hamel was held at the notorious Oranjehotel, where he was interrogated and tortured for weeks. In an astonishing act of resistance, he did not reveal anything about his clients, collaborators, or the broadcasting code. The Germans then arrested Dutch code specialist Henri Koot, but he declared that he was unable to decrypt the messages. It was only when the Germans threatened to charge Van Hamel that Koot revealed Van Hamel had been dropped into the Netherlands from England.

---

[34] The moffen (singular mof) was a derogatory Dutch term for Germans, like the French 'boches', or the English 'krauts'.

The Germans didn't believe Koot until he pointed them to where Van Hamel had buried his parachute. In this way, Koot[35] provided enough information to protect Van Hamel, but he did not provide any further details or names. Koot was released after this incident, but remained under close surveillance. He therefore confined his resistance activities to distributing food parcels, but was still imprisoned for a few weeks in 1944.

Over the course of World War II, the Germans would detain over 25,000 people in the Oranjehotel for interrogation and prosecution, including members of the Dutch resistance, Jews, and Jehovah's Witnesses.

In late October 1940, Jos de Vos received word that Jean Mesritz had reached England. A few days later, however, De Vos was greatly disappointed when he was called to the Houtmanstraat house where Jean's grandmother, Madame Mulder, nervously told him that Jean's attempt to reach England had failed.

On the 27th of November 1940, nearly 4 months after Léo and Ernestine had set sail for the USA, Léo's brother Denis sent a letter to Léo's son-in-law, Charles Béliard, giving the terrible news.

---

[35] Henri Koot, a veteran of WWI, was a leader in Dutch cryptography between the wars. However, he was dismissed as head of the Cryptographic Bureau in 1933, due to budget cuts. In 1937 he was given the rank of Reserve Colonel, and in 1939 was brought in to train other personnel, but it was too late to implement his new code system.

In April 1945, Koot helped avoid a bloodbath by negotiating the German capitulation with German Lieutenant General P. Reichelt — for which role Koot was temporarily promoted to Reserve Major General.

DENIS MESRITZ

GENÉVE 27 Novembre 1940.
5, Av. Gaspard Vallette
Tél. App. 44 670
Tel. Bur. 26 165

My dear Charles,

I hope you have received my letter of the
19th current.

Since then I have received a first letter
from my mother which rather worried me. She told
me that she was very lonely and that I could
understand the reason of her loneliness
from my brother.

Well, last night, I received a new letter
from Grandmother, dated 19 November, which said :
"I told you, fifteen days ago, that I was very
lonely and that Léo would certainly give you
the reasons. My solitude is always the same,
but you will not get the reason from Léo.
It is about Jean. I thought then that from
where he was, he could correspond with his
father. An opportunity to go to England
presented itself, he accepted it, because he
wanted to do all that he could for his country.

./.

But he and his friends were captured
and taken to the prison cells in
Scheveningue.

It was only on the sixth of this
month that I learned about him and his
friends.

I have received a letter from him.
He is allowed to write to me each Sunday
and I can do the same Visits are not allowed.
He is in a cell block and he wrote to me
that I should not worry, because he is in
good health and the food is good."

Grandmother added : He is young and
has done his service, but the situation
is still terrible for him. I pray to God
to let me live long enough to see him again.

So I gather from this letter that Jean,
with some friends, has tried to get to
England but unfortunately he did not
make it.

I don t know if anyone has been able to
write about this to your brother-in-law. I will
leave you to decide whether to let Claire know.

·/.

Could you kindly let me know if you have written about it to your wife and my brother? I know that Grandmother writes regularly to your father-in-law, but she has not told me whether she has informed him of this.

Poor Jean, I feel for him with all my heart, as I feel also for his father.

What do you think of this?

Do you believe that the fact Jean is an officer will increase his sentence? What do you think are his risks? If I get any details I will make sure to let you know them immediately.

I can only agree with Jean's desire to serve his country.

I impatiently await your response and send you, my dear Charles, all my good wishes.

Figure 25: Transcript of letter dated 27 November 1940, from Denis Mesritz (Léo's brother) to Charles Béliard (Léo's son-in-law), giving news of Jean's capture and imprisonment. Translated by Luc Béliard.

Jean's Trial

Months passed before Jean was sent to trial, and he remained at the Oranjehotel until April 1941, when he received his sentence. During his detention, Jean recognised people who came through the prison, including his friend Erik Hazelhoff and his lecturer, **Professor Rudolf Pabus Cleveringa**.

On the 18th of December 1940, **Professor Benjamin Telders**, a fierce resistance fighter and colleague of Professor Cleveringa, had been arrested and imprisoned at the Oranjehotel. He remained there until the 28th of June 1941, so may also have crossed paths with Jean.

On the 2nd of April 1941, Erik Hazelhoff and fellow resistance fighter Paul Renardel had planned to leave the Netherlands for England. Unfortunately, they were both arrested by the Germans. In *Soldier of Orange*, Hazelhoff recalls the earlier arrest of another of the Leidener set, Carel Kranenburg:

> *Carel, meanwhile, sold by Blubber[36] for a few guilders, spent his first night in the Oranjehotel. I never saw him again.*

At the Oranjehotel, Erik realised that Jean and others he knew were also being held there. Thankfully, Erik and Paul regained their freedom after only a few days because, they argued, they were only having a drink. In *Soldier of Orange*, Hazelhoff recounts his arrest and detention at Scheveningen:

---

[36] 'Blubber' was the alias of a contact recruited to supposedly help Hazelhoff get to England. Due to his betrayal, Blubber was executed by the Dutch Underground.

We stopped at a small wooden door beside the main gate of the Oranjehotel. The blind wall stretched the length of the block and around both corners. Through a second entrance we stepped into the building and now the view hit me like a blow — the long, deserted corridors, the shiny, tiled walls, rows of green cell-doors in absolute silence. My heart cramped in my chest; were there really people behind those doors? Then suddenly, like a clarion call, the realisation: Jean is in here! And Lodo! And Carel! And Van Beelen! And Jan and Piet and Dirk and Gerard and Robert — friends, some Leideners [a nickname for those attending Leiden University], all Hollanders, those who had dared to fight and risk, the best! When I walked into my solitary cell, I listened proudly for the crunch of the door behind me.

As Erik Hazelhoff left his cell on the 5th of April 1941, he recalled that, suddenly, someone called his name:

There, at the far end of Hall C, broom and bucket in hand, stood Jean Mesritz. Not another soul was in sight. He put his bucket on the floor, leaned the broom against the wall and stretched both arms into the air as wide as he could, hands open, fingers spread. So, he stood motionless between the blind cell-doors, a warm smile on his face, in a silent, unbelievably exuberant greeting. I waved hurriedly and rushed on, terrified that someone might still recognise me before the prison walls lay behind me.

It would be the last time Erik ever saw Jean.

Two days later, on the 7th of April 1941, the trial of the group caught at Lake Tjeuke — Jean Mesritz, Lodo Van Hamel, Hans

Hers, Marion Smit, Lourens Baas Becking (a Leiden University botany professor), and Jo Allers — was held in the building of the Supreme Court of the Hague. Throughout proceedings, Van Hamel remained steadfast in refusing to give any information. Lodo said, *As a good Dutch officer, I demand the right not to inform the enemy of what could harm the country.*[37]

Jean Mesritz and his fellow prisoners were all found guilty of the various charges against them. Van Hamel was sentenced to death. Lodo's closest colleague, Hans Hers, was sentenced to three years' prison. Jo Allers received a ten-year sentence, but died just 18 months later, on the 12th of October 1943 in Hamelin Prison.

Jean was sentenced to two years of 'Tuchthuis', which was not a straightforward jail, but a 'House of Correction' at either Vught camp or Amersfoort police transit camp. His 'crime' was 'den fortgesetzten Feindbegunstigung', 'continuous favouring of the enemy'. The Germans had started sentencing people using these vague charges as early as 1933. In some Dutch texts, Jean's sentence is described as 'getting into the service of the enemy'. Concrete allegations against Jean are recorded as: helping Lodo van Hamel; donating a staff map of the Hague to Hans Hers (on which Hers pencilled in important military objects); and assisting Hers to bring Van Hamel's suitcase (containing all kinds of incriminating material) to Heerenveen.

On the 16th of June 1941, ten days after his 26th birthday, Lodo van Hamel was executed by firing squad at the Bussumerheide (near Kamp Crailo). His remains were cremated

---

[37] Bernard O'Connor, *Bletchley Park and the Pigeon Spies*, p.57.

Met groote droefheid geven wij kennis van het
bericht van den dood van onzen innig geliefden Zoon,
Broeder, Zwager en Oom

LODEWIJK ANNE RINZE JETSE VAN HAMEL,

Luitenant ter Zee 2e klasse,

26 jaar oud, op 16 Juni l.l.

Baarn, Mariënhof, 19 Juni 1941.

Prof. Mr. J. A. VAN HAMEL.
M. L. VAN HAMEL—DE VRIES FEYENS.

M. L. DE BEAUFORT—VAN HAMEL.
Jhr. W. H. DE BEAUFORT.
WILLEM HENDRIK.

Mr. Dr. G. A. VAN HAMEL.
W. VAN HAMEL—QUARLES VAN UFFORD.
ANNEMIE.

Geen Rouwbeklag.

Eenige en algemeene kennisgeving.

Figure 26: Notice of the death of Lodo Van Hamel, published in *De Telegraaf* on the 21st of June 1941.

in Driehuis-Westerveld, and news of his death appeared in *De Telegraaf* on the 21st of June.

On the day of Van Hamel's execution, Baas Becking and Marion Smit were acquitted and set free.

Jean's Incarceration

In June 1941, Jean Mesritz was transferred from the Oranjehotel to the Penitentiary in Münster, Germany.

At the end of that month, Professor Benjamin Telders was also transferred from the Oranjehotel, but was sent to the Buchenwald concentration camp. The Nazis had established Buchenwald, near Weimar, in July 1937. One of the first and largest concentration camps in Germany, Buchenwald subjected inmates to either slave labour, where many were 'worked to death', or execution, mostly by gunshot or hanging. Many inmates at Buchenwald also died as a result of human experimentation, or fell victim to arbitrary acts perpetrated by the SS guards. Telders endured a hard time there for over two-and-a-half years, until he was sent to Bergen-Belsen concentration camp in January 1944.

Over the course of the war, the Germans ran three main camps in the Netherlands — Westerbork, Vught and Amersfoort — but there were over 50 minor or temporary Nazi camps.

On the 18th of August 1941, Amersfoort camp opened in Eastern Holland. Amersfoort was not a concentration camp, but a large police prison under the command of the Security Police or 'SD'. During its first period of operation, from August 1941 to March 1943, Amersfoort held 8,500 prisoners for various periods, including 'protection inmates' and prisoners waiting for transport to German concentration camps or sentenced to death. Amersfoort was closed from March to June 1943. When it reopened, a further 26,700 prisoners were held there, until they were released or transported to Germany.

When the German city of Münster was bombed by allied air force raids, possibly as early as May 1943, prisoner Jean Mesritz was transferred from the Münster Penitentiary to Kamp Rhede-Brual (also called Brual-Rhede), a peat mining camp near Papenburg.

At Rhede-Brual, prisoners had to work 8 to 10 hours a day collecting heavy peat for local companies and farmers. As the war went on, conditions worsened: hygiene was poor, food was scarce, and prisoners endured significant mental and physical abuse. Many survivors of Rhede-Brual later committed suicide.

Having served his two years' detention, on the night before Jean's release in spring 1943, he was given a railway ticket. The next day, however, the railway ticket was taken from him. Jean was told that he would now be held in 'Schutzhaft' ('protective custody').[38] It was a bitter blow.

On the 5th of June 1943, Jean was brought into the Vught concentration camp. His prisoner card states that he had 'been ill'. At least construction had finished by that time: the first prisoners who arrived at Vught had had to finish constructing the camp. During its operation from January 1943 until September 1944, Vught held nearly 31,000 inmates: Jews, political prisoners, resistance fighters, gypsies, Jehovah's Witnesses, homosexuals, homeless people, black market traders, criminals and hostages. Due to hunger, sickness, and abuse, at least 749 men, women and children died there. Of these, 329 were murdered at the execution site just outside the camp.

In the Hague, on the 29th of June 1943, Madame Mulder — widow of August Mesritz, beloved mother of Léo, and

---

[38] Schutzhaft or 'protective custody' was a para-legal term often used to imprison political opponents, Jews, and other persecuted groups in Nazi Germany. Schutzhaft did not provide for a judicial warrant, and detainees, most often, never saw a judge. Even if they had originally been arrested and acquitted, or had completed their sentence, they could continue to be held under schutzhaft. These prisoners were often sent to concentration camps.

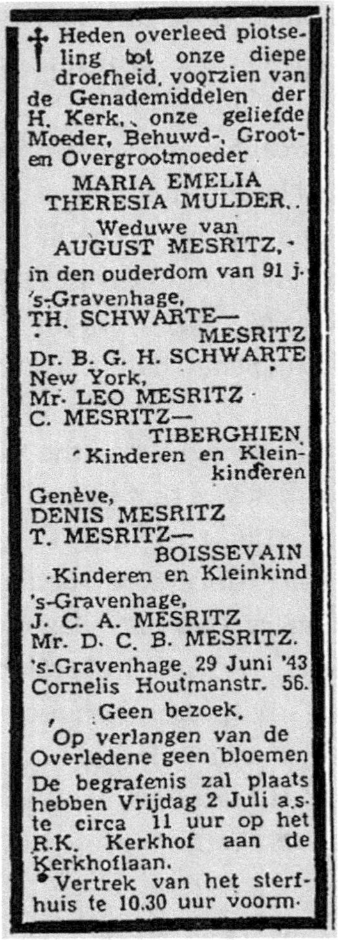

† Heden overleed plotseling tot onze diepe droefheid, voorzien van de Genademiddelen der H. Kerk, onze geliefde Moeder, Behuwd-, Groot- en Overgrootmoeder

MARIA EMELIA THERESIA MULDER,.
Weduwe van
AUGUST MESRITZ, ·
in den ouderdom van 91 j.

's-Gravenhage,
TH. SCHWARTE—
. MESRITZ
Dr. B. G. H. SCHWARTE
New York,
Mr. LEO MESRITZ ·
C. MESRITZ—
TIBERGHIEN
· Kinderen en Klein-
kinderen

Genève,
DENIS MESRITZ
T. MESRITZ—
BOISSEVAIN
·Kinderen en Kleinkind

's-Gravenhage,
J. C. A. MESRITZ
Mr. D. C. B. MESRITZ.
's-Gravenhage, 29 Juni '43
Cornelis Houtmanstr. 56.

. Geen bezoek.
' Op verlangen van de Overledene geen bloemen De begrafenis zal plaats hebben Vrijdag 2 Juli a.s. te circa 11 uur op het R.K. Kerkhof aan de Kerkhoflaan.
· Vertrek van het sterfhuis te 10.30 uur voorm·

Today, to our deep sadness, provided with the means of mercy of the Holy Church, suddenly passed away our beloved mother, wife, grandmother and great-grandmother

Maria Emelia Theresia Mulder,
Widow of August Mesritz,
at the age of 91 years.

The Hague,
TH. SCHWARTE-MESRITZ
Dr. B.G.H. SCHWARTE
New York,
Mr. LEO MESRITZ
C. MESRITZ-TIBERGHIEN
Children and grandchildren.
Geneva,
DENIS MESRITZ
T. MESRITZ-BOISSEVAIN
Children and grandchild
The Hague
J.C.A. MESRITZ
Mr. D.C.B. MESRITZ
The Hague, 29 June 1943
56 Corn Houtmanstraat.

No visitors.
No flowers at the request of the deceased.
The funeral will take place Friday 2nd July at approximately 11 AM at the RK Cemetery on the Kerkhoflaan. Departure from the house of death at 10.30 AM.

Figure 27: Madame Mulder's funeral notice, published in *Het Vaderland*, 1 July 1943. Translated by Helena Bond using Google Translate.

grandmother to Claire, Lucien, Jean and Denis — died. Her funeral notice recorded that both Jean and Denis were registered as residing in the Hague, although we know Jean was being held in Vught at the time.

While in Vught, Jean met fellow political prisoner **Hans van Ketwich Verschuur**. In a letter after the war (dated 27 July 1945) to Jean's friend and relative, **Willem Karel Hendrik Feuilletau de Bruyn**, Van Ketwich Verschuur recalled Jean:

> ... by his personality and his character, his gifts of heart and head, [Jean] had been able to win everyone's sympathy from the start and, therefore, he had quickly acquired a position which avoided him the unpleasant sides of camp life, a camp life, by the way, which, apart from some excesses, was a 'sanatorium' when compared with what Jean would later endure in Germany.

In October 1943, another inmate at Vught, David Koker, recalled a conversation with Jean:

> Have spoken with Jan [who we assume is Jean Mesritz], who is very angry with himself because he didn't reach the other side [meaning the UK]; he could hit himself and thinks about all his comrades who did manage it. "There is no honour in being here," he says.[39]

A new year dawned. In January 1944, Professor Benjamin Telders was sent from Buchenwald concentration camp to Vught. At Vught, Telders was given the opportunity of a study assignment via outside work at Philips. During the spring of 1944, Professor Cleveringa, with a few colleagues, was also sent to Vught camp for joining in with the resistance movement. There, he met his student from before the war, Jean Mesritz. Cleveringa recorded his first moments at Vught and meeting Jean:

---

[39] David Koker, *At the Edge of the Abyss: A Concentration Camp Diary 1943–1944*, p.264.

It started exactly in the way that I already knew from prison in Scheveningen. Several of my fellow sufferers, who were a bit greener at this point, were unpleasantly surprised. There was no lack of shouting, and we had to stand with our faces to the wall. "Looking at paintings" we called that mockingly in Scheveningen. It got too much for one of the Leiden policemen and, at risk of being struck, he protested. Surprisingly, this was indeed successful, and we were allowed to turn around again. Then the officers left and we were told that we had to go with them inside the gate. Thus, we got to see the concentration camp inside for the first time ...

Here I underwent my first personal interrogation by the 'political department' (which was housed in the 'Kommandantur' and which I later got to know very well).

We had to give all kinds of personal details: name, whether we were married and ... finally, whether we had been punished before. Most of my fellow sufferers still had a clean slate, but I had 8.5 months in 'protective custody' in Scheveningen to my name; I was a repeat offender!

Then off to the bathhouse, where we first handed in our money and valuables (watches, rings, fountain pens, pencils, etc.). Here I came face to face with the people who would become my closest friends.

I immediately found myself eye to eye with my student Jean Mesritz, who showed that he immediately recognised me. I didn't recognise him straight away; not even when he reminded me of how we had been together in Scheveningen.

He had been captured in October 1940 at the Tjeukemeer with Baas Becking during a failed crossing to England to enlist in the Dutch army; and he was therefore sentenced to two years imprisonment. He had served that punishment in several prisons in Germany.[40]

On Cleveringa's arrival, Jean offered to help the professor during his time in Vught, and he was true to his word. A grateful Cleveringa wrote afterwards:

I mean, he [Jean] went through a lot of hardship ... The night before he was to have been released, he had already been handed his rail ticket, but on the day itself it had been taken from him again, and he was told that he was now in protective custody. He had been in Vught since the spring of 1943 ... This hard-tested young man was always cheerful and brave, always out to help others, always full of plans for the future! He deserved respect! And the most important thing he said to me was: "Professor, I will help you!" When I answered him, "I have no doubts about your good intentions, but I do doubt your ability", he replied, "You just wait and see!" And he kept his word; he indeed helped me a lot, very much.

In his diary, Professor Cleveringa recorded the procedures regarding hair cutting and shaving at Vught camp, noting the resourcefulness of Jean Mesritz:

---

[40] RP Cleveringa, *Gedenkschriften*. Memoirs written by Cleveringa in Amsterdam 1977 about life as a prisoner in Nazi camps in 1940–41, and again in 1944, including Vught Camp. Translated from Dutch by Tineke Schoonens.

... when I arrived at the camp, I had to hand in my shaving equipment. Fortunately, the unsurpassed Mesritz delivered a razor and some shaving cream. I don't know from where he "organised" it, but he had a knack for it.

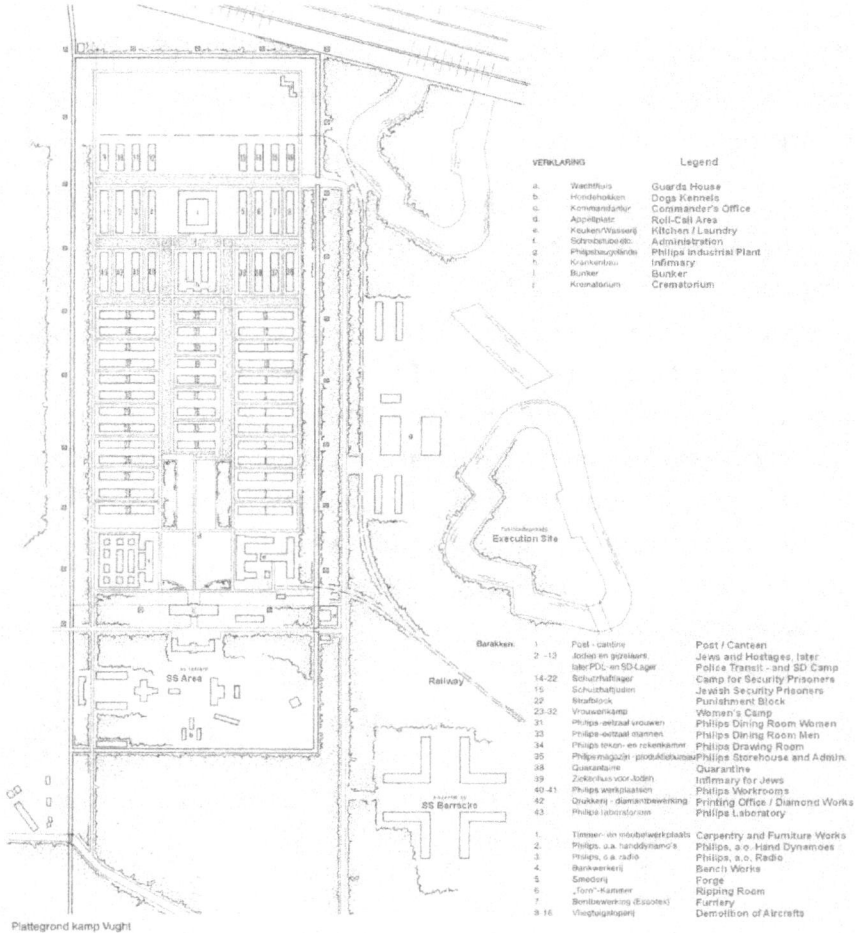

Figure 28: An aerial map of Kamp Vught (Herzogenbusch), which, in 1940, was a 'Tuchthuis' or 'house of correction' in occupied Holland. Vught became an SS concentration camp in January 1943.

Cleveringa also described the food at Vught, and how Jean helped circumvent a ban on parcels to the prisoners in early 1944:

> *At the end of February parcels were banned and the situation became critical for many. This was "thanks to" some women from Soviet who had tried to smuggle in knives, baked into cakes. When this was discovered, the whole cellblock was punished. The parcel ban lasted about 1.5 months. In the meantime, we thought of all sorts of ways to get around this. One thought of this, another of that. The excellent Mesritz helped me. He managed to get a message out to keep sending me parcels, but to his address, and, with the help of his friends at the post office, he collected a second parcel, as well as his. That is how I received my parcels, despite the ban.*

Throughout Jean's imprisonment, **Lize** (his childhood nanny and Madame Mulder's housekeeper) and family friend **Roosje van Lelyveld Furstner** sent parcels to Jean. We know that he received at least some of them, and that they made a significant difference to his life in the camps.

Professor Cleveringa received a pair of mountain boots. In *Gedenkschriften*, he recorded his deliberations about who should get them when he left the camp in June 1944:

> *What a blessing those mountain boots were. They saved me a lot of cold and wetness. In the mud, during evening rollcalls when we sometimes had wet snow, I was dry, and my health would have been much worse without them. Everyone envied those shoes and, when I left, there were lots of interested parties. I hesitated between Duller and Mesritz. Mesritz was younger, Duller was married and had children. Mesritz was no*

longer working with us and was not around when I left. Both
had rendered many and great services, but Duller perhaps the
biggest. Mesritz was bigger than me and Duller had the same
size foot, and so the choice fell on Duller.

At some stage in June 1944, brothers Jean and Denis Mesritz were
both in Vught concentration camp. Jean wrote to their nanny,
Lize, telling her that he had seen his brother in Vught. We do
not know how long Jean and Denis were both there, nor whether
they were able to spend any time with each other. In July, Jean
was sent back to Germany. It seems that the brothers' meeting
was short, probably only a day or two at most, as each prisoner
was part of a different working group, sent to different places.

The 6th of June 1944 was 'D-Day', when the Allies landed
on Normandy beaches. In response, the Germans took 1,500
prisoners to Vught from jail in the Oranjehotel. Between July
and September, 400 Vught prisoners were executed, including
many resistance fighters. As the Allied forces approached, the
camp was evacuated and prisoners transferred to concentration
camps further east.

On the 21st of August, Jean was sent to Westerbork
camp via Zwolle. He was placed in Barrack 67, one of two
'Penitentiary Barracks'. Inside these, prisoners were surrounded
by extra barbed wire and watch towers, and the inhabitants were
not allowed to walk freely about the camp, as other inmates were.

Westerbork, headed by Albert Gemmeker of the SS, was
the oldest and largest camp for Jews, and was used as a staging
ground for deportation. Transport trains arrived at Westerbork
every Tuesday from July 1942 to September 1944, and deported an
estimated total of 97,776 Jews. Jewish inmates were transported

in waves to Auschwitz (65 train-loads, totalling 60,330 people), Sobibor (19 train-loads, totalling 34,313 people), Theresienstadt ghetto (7 train-loads, totalling 4,771 people), and Bergen-Belsen concentration camp (8 train-loads, totalling 3,724 people). The great majority of the 94,643 persons sent to Auschwitz and Sobibor, both in German-occupied Poland, were murdered on arrival.[41]

Kamp Westerbork had a school, orchestra, hairdresser, and even restaurants, designed by SS officials to give inmates a false sense of hope for survival, and to aid in avoiding problems during transportation. Apart from metalwork, farm work and jobs in health services, the camp ran cultural activities in music and stage performances by the inmates. A special, separate work group of 2,000 'permanent' Jewish inmates was used as a camp labour force. Within this group was a sub-group constituting a 'camp police force' who were required to assist with transports and to keep order. The SS actually had very little to do with selecting transferees; this job fell to the inmates of the camp police force. Most 'permanent' inmates were eventually sent to concentration or death camps themselves. Only 5,000 Jews who passed through Westerbork survived.

On the 13th of September 1944, from New York, Léo Mesritz enquired about his son, Jean. That same day, as Jean's prisoner card shows, he was moved from Westerbork to Bergen-Belsen, a journey of more than 270 kilometres east, in a convoy of Jews and half-Jews. His name on the transport list reported Jean as

---

[41] These figures are from 'Camp Westerbork transport schedules', http://www.holocaust-lestweforget.com/westerbork-transport-schedule.html.

a 'Straffaellige Mischlinge'.[42] The text continued that Jean was sentenced to two years in the 'detention centre', and that he should be placed in 'protective custody'.

In *The World of My Past*, Abraham Biderman wrote:

I was now classified as a 'Schutzhäftling' (a prisoner in 'safe custody') ... The veteran prisoners, to cheer us up, told us, "You're better off having a number ... At least they'll keep you alive and eventually you will be assigned to slave labour. Those without numbers are in line to go up in smoke at any moment to keep the furnaces going."

With hindsight, in all respects this train transit was a 'special transport' — it was the final train (and the 102nd) to depart Westerbork. We know the names of 297 people in the train. Also in the train were fifty unnamed children, from babies to ten-year-olds. Arrested in their hiding places, they were forced to survive without their parents. The train's destination was Bergen-Belsen. Jean Mesritz is listed on the registry of prisoners there.

In a diary entry from September 1944, psychiatrist and fellow Westerbork inmate Louis Tas (1920–2011), alias Loden Vogel, described his first impressions of Jean Mesritz in Bergen-Belsen:

I am now lying among the old inmates of Vught, very nice chaps who show a lot of camaraderie among each other and with me: Jean Mesritz reminds me of Kompaan, and a boy, Z., who spent a lot of time with Flap in Vught ...

---

[42] Straffaellige Mischlinge was a derogatory Nazi term used on official records and translated as 'delinquent of mixed origin' or 'delinquent half-Jew'. 'Mischlinge' denoted a person of mixed Aryan and non-Aryan background, and had a derogatory sense, like 'mongrel' or 'half-breed'.

In a further diary entry, dated 28th September, Tas recounted the misfortunes of Jean Mesritz:

> *The first night I had slept cosily with Jean M., who was transported (put on the train) as an Aryan. He [Jean] was haunted by misfortune. The horses' stable had grown into a bad command [a group with a task under German command] where no benefits were to be gained. People wanted to do him [Jean] a favour, but exactly the morning at which they tried to smuggle him into the bread commando, he went to Rau and showed a doctor's note for light work ...*

In a diary entry dated 3rd November 1944, Tas again mentioned Jean, noting his sense of humour:

> *When I asked [Jean] what had been his most unpleasant experience he said: "The worst is when you have worked all day in the rain, a couple of hours longer than you would expect, and suddenly on the way back you happen to make up a majestic joke and you tell it enthusiastically to discover that no one understands ..."*

A letter from fellow prisoner Jacob Asscher Jr[43] to Madame Roosje Furstner mentioned changes at Bergen-Belsen and news of Jean Mesritz:

---

[43] Jacob Asscher Jr. brought the family firm, Amsterdam's Royal Asscher Diamond Company, to international prominence with his patented Asscher cut. During WWII, the family's assets were seized by the Germans, and most of the family and company were imprisoned and murdered as Jews. In addition, Jacob's brother Abraham was required by the Nazis to head a Jewish Council — a role for which he was vilified after the war, though later exonerated.

In early December 1944, he was extended from Belsen as thoroughbred 'Aryan'.

He [Jean] and we were impressed that he had been released and that he could be employed as a free worker.

The other non-Jews who, with him, had been transported to Belsen, were sent on a so-called criminal transport at about the same time. I fear that there will be only a few survivors who will return, as there are hardly any from Belsen either.

On the 15th of December 1944, during the Hunger Winter, Jean Mesritz was transported from Bergen-Belsen to an unknown camp. It is quite possible that the camp was Hannover-Misburg, a satellite camp of Neuengamme concentration camp in Germany. The first prisoners to Hannover-Misburg arrived in late June 1944. They were forced to sleep in tents or holes in the ground until the first huts were completed. These prisoners were used for clearance and construction work at Deurag (a large oil refinery), to repair damage from Allied bombing raids. Hannover-Misburg registered 55 deaths, but the data on this camp is incomplete and the number of victims was certainly higher.

Three 'Cancellation Cards' exist regarding prisoner Jean Mesritz, No: 208209, in response to three separate enquiries from Jean's father, Léo. The first was made as early as the 13th of September, 1944, though the response must have been sent late in the year, or early in 1945, as it says Jean had been *deported to Bergen–Belsen*. Certainly the second enquiry, made on the 19th of December 1946, was not answered until *27 FEB* (the ink has faded, but we can assume the year was 1947), by which time he was

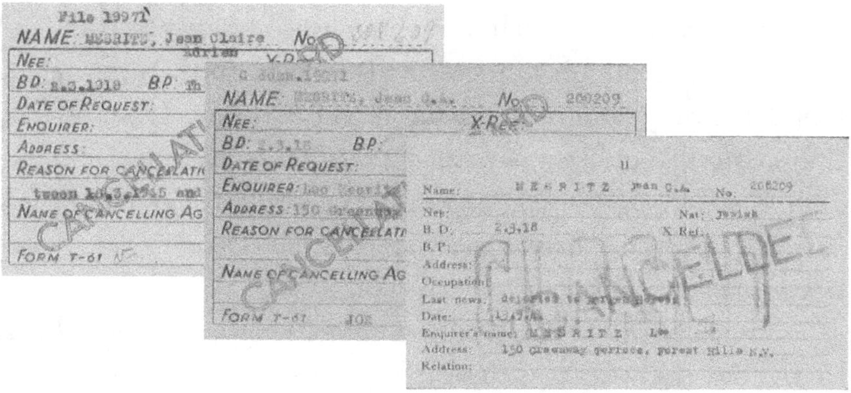

Figure 29: The three Cancellation Cards issued in response to Léo's enquiries.

reported *deceased*. These enquiries were made from Léo's home in Forest Hills, New York.

On the 25th of February 1945, Jean Mesritz was the only Dutch man in a transport of 150 Russians and Poles. He arrived at Neuengamme in a pitiful state: weakened and frail, suffering from dysentery and riddled with lice, after years spent in continual transport and filthy German prisons. Jean told fellow prisoner Van Ketwich Verschuur, whom he had befriended at Vught camp, that the question of his Jewishness was resolved at Westerbork. Jean had been deemed Aryan, not Jewish, yet authorities condemned him to two further years of 'correction', and he had been sentenced to do them.

Jean's Death

In a letter to Jean's relative, Willem Feuilletau de Bruyn, dated the 27th of July 1945, fellow inmate Van Ketwich Verschuur related the circumstances around Jean's final days, and his attempts to protect Jean. Van Ketwich Verschuur was anxious to find Jean a small, sheltered job to recover his health, and wrote that he found a coveted administrative role in the hospital that offered the possibility of *great advantages, facilitating and making life in camp a little more pleasant and where he would therefore probably have fully recovered. I must add that, by camp standards, he was not sick enough to be hospitalised.*

Tragically, *this beautiful project was foiled by a fatal coincidence.* On the day that Jean was to start work, he was transported back to Hannover-Misburg with some 250 other detainees. When Van Ketwich Verschuur found this out, he was unable to get Jean out of the group. He later lamented: *It was unfortunately impossible for me to change anything, something that may sound implausible, but for those who know life in a camp, this is perfectly understandable.*

He continued, *this was a very great disappointment to us both ... I believe we both intuitively felt that Hannover would be fatal for Jean.*

The sad change in Jean's fate was apparently caused by friction between Dutch and Danish inmates at Neuengamme. Dutch prisoners had requested the removal from hospital of Danish inmates who they suspected of faking illness to avoid

Figure 30: Willem Karel Hendrik Feuilletau de Bruyn married Henriëtte Mulder (Madame Mulder's niece).

being transferred. *Some Danish prisoners benefited with clothing and medical supplies from the Danish Red Cross, and came to be considered 'lords' of the camp. With their butter, sausages and smoking articles, they could get away with anything.* After Van Ketwich Verschuur and others intervened, several Danes who had managed to get into hospital to avoid being sent on the transport were evicted from hospital. Unfortunately, Jean was wrongly included with the Danes.

Two weeks later, Van Ketwich Verschuur received heartbreaking confirmation that Jean had died. He blamed himself for not doing more to save Jean. He wrote: *He [Jean] is one of the best of so many other good friends that we had to leave there in Germany.*

Jean's final Cancellation Card states that he *died at Neuengamme betweeen 16.3.1945 and 31.3.1945.* Interestingly, this card gives his nationality as *Dutch,* whereas the first card claimed he was *Jewish.* Accounts from Jean's fellow inmates in all the German camps that he went through say that Jean was always in good spirits, always helping others, and that he had many plans for the future, which earned him their deepest respect.

Jean was buried at Friedhof Maschee, Hanover, according to Red Cross records. He is now remembered, with other Dutch citizens who died in concentration camps, in the Dutch Field of Honour at the Hamburg-Ohlsdorf War Cemetery.

Figure 31: The Dutch Field of Honour at Hamburg-Ohlsdorf Cemetery honours the Dutch who died in German camps, including Jean Claire Adrien Mesritz.

Chapter 5

Denis' Resistance

Denis Mesritz was the youngest of the four children. Imagine Denis as a young boy dressed in a sailor suit, sitting in a child-size armchair ... We know such a scene existed thanks to **Madame Roosje van Lelyveld Furstner**, a family friend, whose notebook from those years has outlived her.

Figure 32: Young Denis in his sailor's outfit.

Figure 33: Friends of the Mesritz family, Madame Roosje van Lelyveld Furstner and her husband, Dr Willem Furstner. (Photo taken in Monte Carlo in 1930.)

The Furstners were close friends of the Mesritz family and, in November 1931, Madame Furstner fondly recalled a day when Léo and Ernestine came to visit her and her son Charles, then a toddler:

The boy was given a small armchair from Ernestine Mesritz that came from their boys, and he was sitting in it every afternoon and drinking his tea next to me.

Charles went upstairs and had been dreaming for weeks to wear a small white sailor's outfit, formerly from Denis Mesritz. He really looked cute and he was very proud in it. We drank tea ...

Fast forward to the age of eighteen, and in 1938, Denis Mesritz enrolled in University. Denis was of a studious nature. We are not sure why he chose to attend Groningen University, rather than Leiden like his father and brother, but he attained a Master of Law (LLM) there, while also working for the Dutch resistance.

At some stage, Denis lived at 33 Jozef Israëlsstraat, Groningen. The house was then known as 'Kakatoe' — we think it was a family house that rented out rooms to students.

In an interesting coincidence, Denis' cousin Denise, daughter of his Uncle Denis, bought a painting by Jozef Israëls, the celebrated Dutch artist after whom the street was named. The painting is a water colour of a girl sitting in the dunes and looking out to sea. She gave the painting to my daughter Denise (her namesake), and our family has enjoyed it for many years.

Denis joined the Groningen Student Association 'Vindicat' in 1939, sponsored by a Mr F Ringers.

Figure 34: 'Kakatoe' — the house at 33 Jozef Israëlsstraat, Groningen, where Denis lived for a while as a law student.

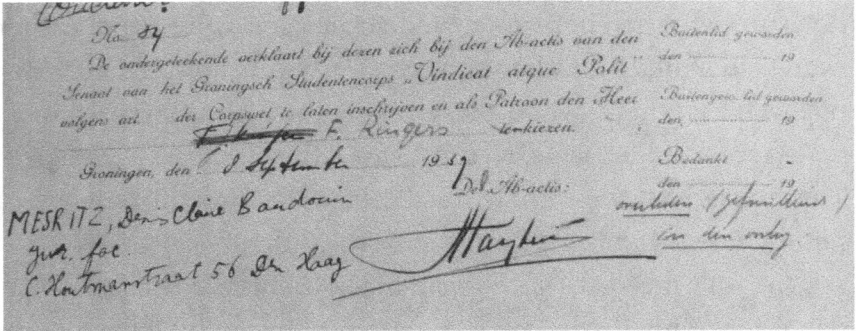

Figure 35: Application for Denis Mesritz to join 'Vindicat', the Groningen Student Association.

On the 15th of May 1940, just five days after Germany invaded the Netherlands, unknown to his father Léo, Denis started working with the Dutch resistance.

The first illegal Dutch resistance pamphlet, *Geuzenbericht*, soon appeared, and by early August 1940 both sons of Léo and Ernestine Mesritz were doing their parts to resist the Nazi occupation. Denis was a key player in establishing the Dutch Student Federation, whose aim was to unite and mobilise all tertiary student organisations.

Organising the student resistance

Academics and students across the country were rebelling against the Nazi occupation. Further south at Leiden University, when presented with the Aryan Declaration to sign in October 1940, Professor of International Law **Benjamin Marius Telders** insisted that fellow academics not sign. He approached the Supreme Court, hoping that his university would oppose the statement. The Council, however, fell in line with the demands of the Nazis.

Telders then succeeded in persuading his colleagues to file a protest with the curators of the university, with a request to pass this protest on to the Acting Secretary-General of the Ministry of Education and Science. In the end, however, the Aryan Declaration statement was signed.

By November, after hearing that Jewish staff at Leiden University were to be fired, Professor Telders organised a protest. At 10 AM on the 26th of November 1940, fellow law lecturer **Professor Rudolf Pabus Cleveringa** delivered his now-famous speech protesting against the Nazi orders to dismiss Jewish colleagues. It was an inspiring address. Students at Delft College and Leiden University held a 48-hour strike in support of their Jewish professors; it was to be the first in a series of strikes against such decrees.

The following day, Leiden students typed out Cleveringa's lecture and circulated it to universities throughout Holland. That afternoon, Cleveringa was arrested and taken to the Oranjehotel. Leiden University and Delft College were subsequently closed down indefinitely by German forces. In December 1940, Professor Telders was also arrested, and joined Jean Mesritz and Cleveringa in the Oranjehotel.

In early 1941, while preparing for his Masters degree at Groningen in the north, Denis returned to the Hague. In a letter to Denis' parents dated the 25th of June 1945, family friend *Jos de Vos* described Denis' contribution to early resistance efforts by Dutch university students:

> *... it was not possible for him to live in the Houtmanstraat house [of Mme Mulder], so I suggested that he take a room at my office, which he did.*

As you know, he was in charge of the Students' Association of the University of Groningen, that is to say, the Christian association. But in 1941 all associations were banned, including the Christian. But it continued to exist in the form of a circle of friends and the presidency was offered to Denis ...

This presidency involved more than one might have thought ... First, assistance to students and former students. Denis worked a great deal for this. He travelled from place to place, carrying out what the Germans considered illegal work, such as assistance to hideouts, distribution of illegal prints, financial aid to people, etc.

He was also involved in the illegal press; I was told that he was the editor of Vrij Nederland [Free Netherland]. *Many times, I urged him to be careful, but he knew very well what he was doing. Hundreds of people are obliged to him.*

Figure 36: Denis Mesritz (centre, behind the deckchair) with a group of friends.

During June 1941, after eight months of inactivity, German authorities reopened Leiden University for a few days. No one seems to know why. That summer, Professor Cleveringa was released from the Oranjehotel. Rather than being deported for extermination — as many Dutch Jews were soon to be — he was freed and paid a pension. But he was dismissed from his university post and no longer allowed to lecture.

By October, Jews remaining in the workplace required special permits, and Jewish students in the Netherlands were no longer allowed to be members of student associations. But the student associations decided that would not mean the end of their contact. They continued to gather in literary salons, at which academics gave lectures.

The Christian Association continued to exist in the form of a 'friends meeting club', with Denis Mesritz as its president. As De Vos wrote to Léo in his letter of the 25th of June: *He [Denis] received many visits to our house, even though I spoke to him about it several times, also in view of the danger he faced ... There were also many telephone communications for him.*

Denis kept up with his post-graduate studies and passed his Masters exam in law in October 1941 to become 'Meester'[44] Mesritz. He stayed on in Groningen for additional, practical postgraduate training. Denis most likely wanted to become a lawyer, and to achieve that, he needed to work as a Meester

---

[44] Written as 'Mr' in Dutch, 'Meester' is the title for someone who has finished law school at a university in Holland. The title Mr opens the possibility to write a thesis and a PhD. Once promoted to PhD, the graduate can add Dr to his/her name.

and be admitted to the Bar. Although Denis took his exams at Groningen University, records state that he is from the Hague.

Throughout the war, Groningen University — unlike Leiden University — remained open, but it was slowly assimilated into the national socialist (fascist) administration. During the autumn of 1940, Jewish lecturers were fired, and by the following March, Jewish students were no longer allowed.

When the Keitel (Night and Fog) Decree came into force in December 1941, resistance became illegal. It was clear to both professors and students that attempts at legal, above-ground resistance, which involved public protest, almost always came to nothing. Under the new decree, persons 'endangering German security' (undertaking resistance activities) in German-occupied territories could now be arrested, tried by 'special courts', and either shot or transported to concentration camps.[45]

The Council of Nine

In January 1942, Leidener **Gustave Henri (Han) Gelder** discussed with Utrecht student **Willem (Wim) Eggink** the possibility of forming a consultative body for students of higher education, which would maintain contact at the inter-academic level. Dr Brouwer became the key stimulator of this project.

In March, Denis Mesritz and other members of the academic Dutch resistance formed this new illegal body: the 'Council of Nine'. Comprising representatives from the nine cities where Dutch universities or technical colleges were located, the council

---

[45] 'Night and Fog Decree', *Encyclopaedia Britannica*. www.britannica.com/topic/Night-and-Fog-Decree.

represented their 15,000 students and aimed to lead the student resistance. Denis was a key member of the Council of Nine, and both he and Han Gelder became foremen, coordinating the student resistance. Other members included *Jos van Hövell* and *Anton van Velsen,* both from Dutch noble families who lived in the Hague, and actor and drama teacher *Bob Oosthoek.*

During autumn 1942, Denis, Gelder and Van Hövell agreed that it was desirable to centralise the resistance. In the final months of the year, they contacted Van Velsen, who was living in the Hague. They consulted about coordinating resistance efforts, and Van Velsen involved his friend, Lambertus Neher,

Figure 37: Gustaaf Henri (Han) Gelder (left) and Willem (Wim) Eggink (right), founded the Council of Nine. Both also worked on the illegal resistance paper, *Ons Volk,* and Eggink also on *Het Parool.*

in the initiative. The group formed the National Committee of Resistance (NC) to engage the various academic Dutch resistance groups, which had only limited success as a coordinating agency, but nonetheless did some valuable work in establishing an illegal telephone network. By that time, Denis Mesritz was very involved in the work of the Council of Nine.

Two illegal student papers, *De Geus* and *De Vrije Katheder*, helped to coordinate resistance efforts. *De Geus* had been founded two years earlier by the **Drion brothers**. Initially intended as a newsletter for students, by September 1942 *De Geus* had developed into an opinion-forming magazine and the mouthpiece of the Council of Nine. Now printed and distributed in much larger numbers and reaching the majority of university students, *De Geus* announced the council's existence to the outside world and aimed to provide reliable information and guidance, giving everyone certainty that they were not alone. After the establishment of the Council of Nine, a Groningen edition of *De Geus* also appeared regularly, often printed in the house of a professor whose son devoted himself entirely to this work, under the guidance of *the courageous illegal worker and recently graduated Meester Denis Mesritz*.[46]

Huib Drion, in his well-known 1944 essay 'The romantic roots of democracy', dedicated his observations to his friend Denis Mesritz, whom he described as the liaison between the leaders of the student resistance, the 'Council of Nine', and the periodical *De Geus*:

---

[46] Cited in Vereniging van Groningse Oud-Illegale Werkers. *Hoe Groningen Streed [How Groningen Fought]*. pp 166–188. Translated by Tineke Schoonens.

*Mesritz was a first-rate man, who dedicated himself completely
in his underground work ... A rare, incorruptible and sensitive
man who made an enormous contribution to the resistance.*

Despite the dangers, on the 14th of October 1942 Dutch resistance group members raided a Nazi distribution office. The booty of rationing stamps, coupons, and cards was distributed through LO channels to aid people in hiding. Three days later, the Nazis executed more hostages to 'punish' the Dutch resistance.

This was when the LO formed its vigilante division — the Landelijke Knokploegen (LKP) — which specialised in targeted acts of sabotage, raids on administrative and distribution offices for vital supplies such as food stamps and the means to forge identity documents, and even occasional assassinations.

On the 9th of December, the Secretary General, in cooperation with the Head of Department of Higher Education, Optenoort (an anti-Semite), called the Rectors Magnifici of all Dutch universities and colleges (similar to the Vice-Chancellors of Australian universities) to meet in Amsterdam. The academics were told that 45,000 Dutch workers, including at least 6,000 students, possibly as many as 8,000, would be called up to work in Germany before the 1st of January 1943. It would mean closing all Dutch universities.

The Council of Nine called a protest strike. This news also coincided with the appointment of Anton Mussert (a prominent Dutch fascist) as leader of the Dutch people, and general conscription was expected as a result. Very little came of the strike, which Groningen University did not even join because of its early holiday period. However, the Faculty of Law and Natural Philosophy at Groningen unanimously decided to resign if it came to that, and all faculties sent a letter to the Secretary General with a serious warning and protest.

It was becoming increasingly clear that the occupying forces were preparing a general mobilisation of young workers. The Council of Nine therefore advised the students, many of whom had gone into hiding, to return to their universities and make use of every moment left for study and mutual contact.

Denis Mesritz played a key role in developing a warning system, working with Pieter (Piet) Oosterlee. They set up a network based on a division of the city into districts and neighbourhoods, through which news was passed from person to person so that, apart from those in the top group, each individual knew only a small section of the network.

By mid-January 1943, the Allied conference at Casablanca was demanding the unconditional surrender of Axis powers. In the Netherlands that month, an interview took place regarding the National Committee of Resistance. Those present included Van Velsen, **Van den Bosch**, Andrée Wiltens (an Utrecht law student) and Denis Mesritz. The following month, Denis, Jos van Hövell and Han Gelder were taken on as protégés by Van Velsen. However, the National Committee did not grow into an umbrella organisation as planned, rather, it developed into a separate resistance group, although many of its members were closely involved with other illegal groups.

The Nazis Act Against Students

On the afternoon of the 6th of February 1943, in a laboratory of Groningen University, the telephone rang. A professor answered, only to drop the receiver in terror a moment later. Messages flew back and forth, and people looked for each other in dismay, consulting one another hurriedly. By 4 o'clock that afternoon, all professors and students knew the news: the lecture halls and libraries in Amsterdam, Delft, Wageningen and Utrecht had been raided, and a few hundred students taken and transported under strict guard to the concentration camp in Vught. This was a relatively small number, because it was a Saturday, but everyone feared that worse was to come. Three days later, on the 9th of February, it was a great relief to all when the arrested students were released.

In Groningen, there were only four arrests, which were not proven to be connected to the wider university action. The Groningen business community pledged strong financial support to the professors, if they were forced to resign. Groningen professors met over a weekend and decided that no lectures would be given, nor exams held. In addition, students across the country started boycotting any lectures that were still on.

Nazis and their sympathisers tried to whip up anti-student sentiment. In a speech in the Town Square of Amsterdam, Dutch fascist leader Mussert declared that "*the loafing slags of 20 to 26 years of age should also go to work.*" Fritz Schmidt, the German Commissioner-General for Political Affairs and Propaganda in the occupied Netherlands told a Congress of National Socialists that "*The plutocrats' sons of the dead should be put on the right path in a concentration camp.*" These statements provided a chilling indication of the Germans' motives for the deportation of students.[47]

---

[47] Cited in Vereniging van Groningse Oud-Illegale Werkers. *Hoe Groningen Streed [How Groningen Fought]*. pp 166–188. Translated by Tineke Schoonens.

On the 13th of March 1943, the occupiers brought in a 'Declaration of Loyalty', which all university students were required to sign to remain students. In part, the Declaration read:

> *The undersigned, ... residing in the Netherlands, solemnly declares that he will observe the laws, regulations and other orders in force in the occupied Dutch territory to the best of his knowledge and will refrain from any action directed against the German Empire, the German Wehrmacht, or the Dutch authorities, as well as from any action or behaviour which, in view of the prevailing circumstances, might endanger public order at the establishments of higher education.*[48]

A mere 10% of students signed the document, and all tertiary education came to a halt. It was a symbolic but costly victory, however, because all who refused to sign were required to report for labour duty in Germany. Some then signed, in vain, some reported for labour duty, and the rest of the students went into hiding. After the war, people drew a clear-cut line: if you had signed the Declaration of Loyalty, you had supported the wrong side during the war and, for a while, signatories were banned from receiving any further education.

On the 30th of April, there was a nationwide strike. The Germans retaliated by executing over 200 strikers. Nonetheless, directives from representatives of the Council of Nine were complied with by more than 90% of students. Students held in Vught were not forgotten — of the almost 600 student

---

[48] Cited in Rob Herber, *Nico Bloembergen: Master of Light*, p.88.

prisoners, over 100 were released and every effort was made to get the remainder released.

Following the death of his grandmother in June 1943, Denis moved into her house on Houtmanstraat. Jean, of course, could not join him there, as he was in Vught camp. *Lize*, the young men's nanny and long-time housekeeper for Madame Mulder, took very good care of Denis while he was there, and also supported Jean by visiting and sending him parcels whenever she could.

On the 26th of June 1943, British Prime Minister Churchill assured the people in occupied countries that they would get help before autumn. With this assurance, the Dutch resistance against German occupation grew in strength. Many who had been passive resisters became actively involved, while the ranks of refuge-seekers swelled. German countermeasures often failed, as members of the resistance proved very resourceful. By now, however, the Nazis had rounded up all the Jews they had been able to find, totalling at least 107,000 people. Next, they began picking up any able-bodied men to send as slave labour to concentration camps. Despite this, the steady, albeit slow, advance of the Allies gave the Dutch hope that, one day soon, they would be free of their tormentors.

Resistance Press

During the summer of 1943, discussions between university students and recent graduates led to the development of a new illegal periodical that could reach a Dutch mass readership through a large circulation and a popular style. The goal was to stimulate the spirit of resistance.

In October, making use of contacts obtained through all kinds of resistance activities, Han Gelder, Wim Eggink and Denis Mesritz published the first edition of *Ons Volk* (*Our People*). It was the first resistance publication to include many current photos. The paper was especially useful due to the 'insider information' it shared from within government circles. Ample room was also made for humour, in words and drawings. They printed 55,000 copies and distributed *Ons Volk* throughout the Netherlands, bringing extra risk to its publishers.

Just a little later, on the 15th of October 1943, Denis and **Arthur Meerwaldt** also published the first edition of resistance journal *De Toekomst* (*The Future*). This magazine was published once or twice a month, by the same group as *Ons Volk*, with a print-run of 5,000–10,000 copies. In addition, Denis Mesritz and Arthur Meerwaldt actively participated in producing the resistance papers *Bron*, *De Geus* and later, *Het Parool*. On the 27th of September 1943, it was *Het Parool* that revealed the existence of gas chambers in concentration camps.

During the autumn of 1943, Italy surrendered and the Allies took Naples. But they had still not arrived in the Netherlands.

On the 21st of January 1944, Han Gelder was working in a printshop in the Wouwermanstraat 13, the Hague, when the SiPo (Security Police)[49] conducted a raid on the *Het Parool* newspaper. Gelder, afraid that he might reveal secrets during interrogation, drew his pistol and shot himself through the head. Since he had

---

[49] Sicherheitspolizei or 'SiPo' were the German security police during the Nazi era who carried out state political and criminal investigations. Criminal investigations were carried out by the Kriminal Polizei ('Kripo' for short).

No. 1   7 OCT. 1943

ONS VOLK

DEN VADERLANT GHETROUWE

TER INLEIDING.

„Ons Volk" wil trachten te voorzien in de grote behoefte aan een goede voorlichting, die hier te lande ondanks de uitstekende illegale pers nog steeds bestaat.

Wij denken hierbij vooral aan de arbeiders en de middenstand: het is vooral tot hen, dat wij bij herhaling het woord zullen richten. Wij willen bijdragen tot het aanwakkeren van ons verzet tegen den bezetter enerzijds, tot bewustmaking van de hoge waarden waar wij voor strijden anderzijds. Een zeer belangrijk aandeel in een Geallieerde overwinning kan geleverd worden door de volken in de door den vijand bezette gebieden. Hun taaie en harde, eensgezinde verzet tegen den Duitsen overweldiger, die de oorlog voor een groot deel voert met door hén geleverde wapenen, machines, levensmiddelen en grondstoffen, met gebruikmaking van h u n mensenmateriaal, kan de doorslag geven en de directe oorzaak zijn van een snelle Geallieerde overwinning. „Ons Volk" zal er toe mede kunnen werken om dit besef levendig te houden...

Ernstig dient gewaakt te worden tegen een voorbarig optimisme en een onderschatting van den

DE MEISTAKING

EEN KEERPUNT IN ONZE VERZETSSTRIJD.

Een nabeschouwing.

Op 30 April kondigde de Duitsche Weermachtsbevelhebber een rechtstreeks uit Berlijn toegezonden order af, waarin de Nederlandsche militairen, die reeds bijna drie jaren gedemobiliseerd waren, plotseling op een kennelijk voorwendsel weer in krijgsgevangenschap werden geroepen. Dit bevel werkte als een grove uitdaging en het raakte niet alleen de trots van alle Nederlanders, dat hierdoor de „jongens", die in de Meidagen van 1940 alles voor het Vaderland hadden over gehad, rechtstreeks werden getroffen, maar bovendien zagen honderdduizenden hierdoor hun krat winners in gevaar, om nog maar te zwijgen van de tienduizenden, die zich thans zelf door de afzondering, de verveling en de ontbering van een Duits gevangenkamp bedreigd zagen.

Opmerkelijk was de afwijking van de tot nu toe gevolgde politiek der bezetters, om elke maatregel zo stapje voor stapje, zo geruisloos en met zoveel mogelijkheden van uitzondering door te voeren, dat een duidelijk gesloten front daartegenover moeilijk te voeren en het juiste ogenblik van verzet bijna niet te bepalen was.

Een golf van geestdrift ging dan ook op de 31ste April door het land, toen van steeds meer kanten het bericht kwam: „Twente staakt!", „De mijnen liggen stil!", „De beren in het Noorden leveren geen melk meer!", „De hoogovens liggen plat!" De ren stak de ader aan: in het Noorden, in Twente, in Zwolle en Arnhem, in Brabant en Limburg heerste weldra een vrijwel algemene staking, tal van grote bedrijven in Noord- en Zuid-Holland staakten eveneens; grote verzekeringskantoren, ja deftige departementen, waar enkele jaren tevoren iemand, die over een staking zou hebben gesproken, onmiddellijk voor gek zou zijn verklaard, liepen in de tijd van enkele mi-

vijand. Zeker, de Duitsers hebben gedurende het laatste jaar nederlaag na nederlaag geleden. het Russische front kraakt in al zijn voegen, de duikbootoorlog is verloren, Italië heeft gecapituleerd. Maar nog is het Beest niet verslagen. Nóg kunnen zij, al is het met prijsgeven van uitgestrekte gebieden, al zijn zij volkomen in de verdediging gedrongen, lange tijd doorvechten. Dit moet voor

ons een aansporing zijn om niet te verslappen in ons aller strijd, om met verbeten woede dóór te zetten en het uiterste van onze krachten te vergen.

„Ons Volk" zal er toe mede werken om het verzet tegen den gehaten indringer te verscherpen en tot het uiterste op te voeren, totdat de dag der eindoverwinning is aangebroken.

Figure 38: The first edition of the resistance publication *Ons Volk* was released on 7 October 1943. Denis also worked on *De Geus*, *De Toekomst*, *Bron*, and *Het Parool*.

no identity papers with him, his identity remained hidden. After the war, Han Gelder and his close colleague Denis Mesritz were two of 95 recipients of the Dutch Cross of Resistance. Gelder is now buried in the Dutch Field of Honour at Loenen.

During that raid on *Het Parool* staff, Arthur Meerwaldt fell into German hands. He was imprisoned in the Oranjehotel where he underwent a lengthy interrogation and torture. Denis Mesritz, at just 25 years of age, took over management of the editorial staff of *Ons Volk*.

The Search for Denis

In February 1944, the Germans searched the Houtmanstraat house of the late Madame Mulder, looking for Denis. But he had been forewarned, so he was not there. When the police came looking, housekeeper Lize kept her nerve and gave no indication of his whereabouts. The Germans stayed in the house for two or three days to see if Denis would return. When he did not, they gave up and left.

After the house raid, Denis moved to Haarlem, west of Amsterdam, into the flat of friend and fellow resistance fighter, Jos van Hövell. Denis continued his work in charge of the editorial staff of *Ons Volk* for a few months. During this time, his advisor and friend Jos de Vos met with Denis several times. In his letter of the 25th of June 1945, De Vos wrote that he had again urged Denis to be extremely careful. The Allied invasion in the West had begun and, as the Italians had signed an armistice with the Allies, Denis said to de Vos:

"... now that the [Allied] invasion has started, everyone is needed to properly end this war, so I have to stay at my post."

Denis' Arrest

On the 16th of May 1944, Denis was arrested on an Amsterdam train heading to the Hague. He had travelled to Leiden to meet with Professor of Civil Law, Huib Drion. As usual, to avoid arrest, he was travelling on a false identity card, this time in the name of Vermeer or Van Der Meer, as an employee of the Forestry Department. Unfortunately, however, his papers were missing a control stamp, and this was enough to raise the suspicion of inspectors.

Denis was taken to the Oranjehotel, where guards brought him face to face with his childhood nanny, housekeeper, and now friend, Lize. She had the presence of mind to tell the Germans that she did not know the man in front of her — that he was not Mr Mesritz. As a result, the Germans were not able to confirm that they had captured Denis Mesritz. In his letter of the 25th of June 1945 to Denis' parents, Jos de Vos explains the significance of Lize's actions, writing that, if the Germans had been able to prove Denis' identity: *the chance of getting out of the hands of the 'boches'*[50] *would have been zero.*

Although Denis was arrested for his membership of the National Committee, an illegal organisation, the Germans were never able to prove his identity as a resistance leader. If they

---

[50] 'Boches' is a derogatory French term for Germans, in use since at least WWI; similar to the Dutch derogatory term 'moffen' or the English 'krauts'.

Jozef Felix Henri Marie Baron van Hövell van Wezeveld en Westerflier
Geb. 12 Jan. 1919

Jur. Student – Had zitting in den „Raad van Negen" van het Studentenverzet – Richtte o.a. met Mr. Mesritz in 1943 het „Nationaal Comité van Verzet" op – Gearresteerd 27-3-1944 in een huis waar een Joden-razzia werd gehouden – Van dien dag tot 1-6-1944 in het „Oranjehotel" gezeten – Vervoerd naar Vught, Oranienburg, kamp Neuengamme en Meppel – Neuengamme, aldaar 3-1-1945 overleden –

Figure 39: Leiden student Baron Jozef Felix Henri Marie van Hövell van Wezeveld en Westerflier (Jos van Hövell) was both friend and colleague to Denis Mesritz.

had, it would almost certainly have led him to being tortured and then shot. Instead, in June 1944, Denis was moved to the Vught concentration camp.

At Vught, Denis crossed paths with his brother Jean. We don't know if they were able to meet or just send messages. We do know that Denis told Jean how well Lize had been looking after him at the Houtmanstraat house. Sadly, we have no record of whether the brothers were able to spend any time together. As far as we know, this was the last time the brothers' paths crossed before they died.

De Toekomst never became a major resistance paper, but it filled a niche for a time. After Denis' arrest, Jan Drion stepped up as Chief Editor, and went on to write many articles. Arthur Meerwaldt and Glastra van Loon stepped in as replacement editors, with Heeres and De Groot also working in the team.

On the 22nd of August 1944, **Bob Oosthoek**, a key figure in the resistance and member of the Council of Nine with Denis was arrested and taken to the Oranjehotel, where he was tortured so badly that he was left partially paralysed.

During August and early September, the Allies began closing in on the Netherlands, while the Nazis made a last stand.

Sometime in September, Denis was sent from Vught to Rathenau (sometimes spelt Rathenow), a subcamp of Sachsenhausen, the main concentration camp for the Berlin area. It may have happened on the 5th or 6th of September, when the Nazis transported large numbers of prisoners to Germany, including Professor Benjamin Telders, who was sent to Sachsenhausen.

By the end of September, the Vught camp was liberated, evacuated and closed down. In total, 13,000 men and women had been imprisoned there during the Nazi occupation of the Netherlands, and 450 resistance fighters were executed there. When the Allies reached Vught, they found about 500 dead bodies in piles near the gates, executed the very morning that the camp was liberated. About 500–600 prisoners survived; they had been due to be executed that afternoon.

Denis' Incarceration

Unlike Jean, there is no trace of Denis to be found at Kamp Westerbork, so it is possible that Denis was not brought to Germany via Westerbork, but was sent straight to Rathenau–Sachsenhausen. Located near the German town of Oranienburg, 35 kilometres north of Berlin, Sachsenhausen was a purpose-built concentration camp, which primarily held political prisoners from 1936 to May 1945. Some 30,000 inmates died there from exhaustion, disease, malnutrition, and pneumonia. Many others were executed or died as the result of brutal medical experimentation. Over 100 Dutch resistance fighters were executed at Sachsenhausen.

The subcamp of Rathenau, where Denis was held prisoner, was built in the summer of 1944. Secured with a double row of electrically charged barbed wire fences and five wooden watchtowers, the barracks contained around 500–800 prisoners, most of whom had come from the Netherlands, Belgium, France, Poland, and the Soviet Union. The men were used as forced labour building aircraft, mainly wings, in brutal twelve-hour shifts, seven days a week.

Defeat of Nazi Germany is in Sight

After D-Day in June 1944, Allied forces continued to push German forces back through fierce fighting, with the loss of many lives. The Allies also ordered railway sabotage in the occupied Netherlands. On the 4th of September, Belgium regained its freedom, and the Belgian government returned home from exile. Many of the Nazi occupation forces and their Dutch collaborators fled for Germany on 'Mad Tuesday' (the 5th of September), and American troops crossed the Dutch–Belgian border and freed the town of Maastricht on the 13th and 14th of September.

Crossing the rivers and waterways that run east to west through the Netherlands was a major challenge for the Allied forces, as the Germans held all the bridges. Many soldiers and civilians died in battles across the southern Netherlands and critical infrastructure was damaged.

In the Hunger Winter of 1944–1945, fighting reached the Hague, with V-weapons[51] fired near and over the city. In his letter to Léo Mesritz of the 25th of June, Jos de Vos described these weapons as *appalling things ... which we, the inhabitants of the Hague, carried on the nerves. Five minutes from our office, this V weapon was fired regularly, so that we could see the air forces continuously in action ... which was painful. In the end, there was even a danger of death.*

---

[51] V-weapons, known in German as Vergeltungswaffen (reprisal weapons), were long-range artillery used for strategic bombing, particularly aerial bombings, during World War II. Part of the range of so-called Wunderwaffen (wonder weapons) of Nazi Germany, V-weapons were primarily used to bomb Allied cities , particularly London and Antwerp. They killed approximately 18,000 people, mostly civilians, according to Wikipedia.

De Vos went on to describe how, on the 1st of March 1945, the Mesritz family home at number 56 Houtmanstraat was seriously damaged, and Lize had to leave: *She had just taken steps to empty the house when, on March 3, there was a bombing that destroyed most of the Bezuidenhout district. The property at 56 Houtmanstraat was completely devastated. Everything burned; nothing remained.*

Although the Allies were making ground, Nazi reprisals against Dutch resistance leaders continued. In the first week of January 1945, Arthur Meerwaldt, editor of the Dutch Resistance magazines and close collaborator of Denis, was killed in Eschershausen, a subcamp of Buchenwald. Two weeks later, on the 27th of January, during a meeting of the National Work Committee in Amsterdam, the SiPo raided the address and arrested resistance leader **Walraven van Hall**. Van Hall was locked up in the House of Detention at Weteringschans in Amsterdam.

On the 12th of February 1945, in retaliation for an attack on a member of the Nazi military police, Van Hall, among others, was executed by gunshot. Their bodies were collected and buried in the dunes at Overveen, on the mid-west coast of Holland. Van Hall was later moved to the Honorary Cemetery in nearby Bloemendaal.

Operation Veritable had begun, with 300,000 British, Canadian and Polish soldiers fighting to push the Axis powers back into Germany. The eastern and northern provinces were liberated first, with Germany keeping control in the Netherlands' western provinces until May, when they were finally forced to surrender.

Denis' Death

Exhausted and sick as a result of heavy labour and neglect, on the 17th of March 1945, Denis Mesritz died in Rathenau camp. A statement by an AJ Andrée Wiltens on the 3rd of November 1947 confirmed Denis' death:

> ... and Mesritz (Denis) who was caught in May 1944 and was transported via Vught to Germany, where he perished in the winter in a camp. [52]

In a letter from Léo's brother Denis Mesritz in Switzerland to my father, Charles Béliard, Denis mentioned that his two nephews, Denis and Jean, had met in Kamp Vught, and that they had both been transferred to camps in Germany. He added that they knew through a friend that Denis had been doing 12-hour days of forced labour in a factory near Rathenau. He wrote: *Under-fed and completely exhausted, he [Denis] died on the 17 March, 24 hours after having been transported to a hospital space.*

In March 1949, Denis Mesritz was reburied in the Dutch Field of Honour, at Loenen, Apeldoorn, section E, number 85. Of the 350 Dutchmen so honoured, many were Jean's and Denis' colleagues and friends. Mr PJ Enk, Rector Magnificus of the University of Groningen, Mr Huib Drion, and **Dr W Feuilletau de Bruyn** spoke at Denis' graveside.

Denis was also posthumously awarded the Dutch Cross of Resistance for his work throughout the war.

---

[52] AJ Andrée Wiltens. 'Statement of Wiltens made on November 3, 1947.' Courtesy of NIOD.

Figure 40: Gates to the Dutch Field of Honour at Loenen in Apeldoorn, where Denis was reburied.

Mr. Denis C. B. Mesritz herbegraven

Zaterdagmiddag is het stoffelijk overschot van mr. Denis C. B. Mesritz, dat indertijd van Ratenau naar Amersfoort is overgebracht, op de centrale begraafplaats te Loenen (Veluwe) herbegraven. Mr. Denis Mesritz, wie tijdens de regering van koningin Wilhelmina het verzetskruis posthuum is toegekend, is in de bezettingstijd o.a. illegaal voorzitter van de (ontbonden) Nederlandse Studentenvereniging geweest en medewerker van de Haagse illegale Paroolgroep.

Aan de groeve hebben dr. P. J. Enk, rector magnificus der Groningse universiteit, mr. H. Drion en dr. W. Feuilletau de Bruijn het woord gevoerd.

MR. D.C.B. MESRITZ
VERZETSKRUIS

16.11.1919   19.3.1945

85

Figure 41: Left: Denis' reburial at Loenen was announced in *Het Parool* on 29 March 1949. Right: A simple headstone marks his final resting-place.

Chapter 6

War's End

The final battles of World War II in Europe took place in late April and early May 1945. On the 8th of April 1945, as German surrender to the Allies appeared imminent, Misburg-Hannover concentration camp was closed, and all surviving prisoners were sent to Bergen-Belsen. When the British liberated Bergen-Belsen on the 15th of April, they found almost 60,000 prisoners. Fourteen days later, American troops entered the Dachau camp, where they found thousands of emaciated survivors, and thousands of corpses. Due to the prisoners' poor physical condition, thousands more died soon after liberation.

Allied forces took large numbers of Axis prisoners. On the Western Front, Allies took 1.5 million prisoners, and they captured at least 120,000 German troops in the last campaign of the war in Italy. In the few months up to the end of April, over 800,000 German soldiers surrendered on the Eastern Front. On the 28th of April, Mussolini was executed; the following day, German forces in Italy surrendered. On the 30th of April, Adolf Hitler committed suicide in his bunker.

On the 4th of May 1945, German forces surrendered in Berlin, Denmark, and the Netherlands. At 1600 hours on the 5th of May

1945, General Blaskowitz, the German Commander-in-Chief in the Netherlands, surrendered to Canadian General Foulkes in the Dutch town of Wageningen, in the presence of Prince Bernhard (acting as Commander-in-Chief of the Dutch Interior Forces).

Following news of the German surrender, spontaneous celebrations erupted all over the world on the 7th of May. The following day, the 8th of May 1945, General Keitel signed the general surrender in Germany. The 8th of May became known as Victory in Europe Day, or VE-Day for short, celebrating the formal acceptance by World War II Allied Forces of Germany's unconditional surrender of its armed forces. While many Allied countries observe VE-Day, the Dutch continue to celebrate on the 5th of May, as this date marked the liberation of the Netherlands.

World War II continued in the Pacific, reaching its bitter end on the 2nd of September 1945, after the US dropped two atomic bombs on the Japanese cities of Hiroshima and Nagasaki, killing 100,000 to 200,000 civilians.

Accolades for Jean and Denis

Jean and Denis Mesritz both died in Nazi-run camps in March 1945, just weeks before the end of the war. Although we cannot verify their exact dates of death, records state that Jean died in Neuengamme and Denis died in Rathenau.

After the war, family members Henriëtte Feuilletau de Bruyn-Mulder and her husband placed a death notice about the boys in the paper.

Their parents, Léo and Ernestine, had left Europe for the US on the 4th of August 1940, and we have no record of

Wij ontvingen de droeve tijding, dat in den strijd voor de vrijheid van het Vaderland zijn overleden Jean Mesritz in Maart 1945 in het Aussenkommando Hannover van het concentratiekamp Neuengamme, oud 27 j. en zijn jongere broeder Mr. Denis Mesritz, op 17 Maart 1945 in het concentratiekamp te Rathenau, oud 25 jaar. Namens de familie: Dr. W. K. H. Feuilletau de Bruyn; H. E. Feuilletau de Bruyn-Mulder.	We received the sad news that in the struggle for the freedom of the Fatherland Jean Mesritz died in March 1945 in the Hannover external subcamp of the Neuengammme concentration camp, aged 27, and his younger brother Mr Denis Mesritz, on 17 March 1945 in the concentration camp in Rathenau, aged 25 years. On behalf of the family: Dr WKH Feuilletau de Bruyn; HE Feuilletau de Bruyn-Mulder.

Figure 42: Newspaper notice of Jean and Denis' deaths in *Het Parool*, 17 July 1945. HE is Henriëtte Emma, the niece of Madame Mulder (and therefore Jean and Denis' second cousin). Translation: Dini Elting.

communications between the brothers and their parents after that date. We do know that Léo made numerous attempts to find out what had happened to Jean during and after the war, and he received reports of his sons from their friend and mentor Jos de Vos. Because De Vos gathered news of the young men throughout the war, it is possible that Léo heard updates through him.

After their deaths, in a letter dated the 25th of June 1945 to Léo and Ernestine Mesritz, De Vos expressed his deep admiration for Jean and Denis, and offered comfort:

> You know that I have known the boys since their birth and that they are in my thoughts at all times. I would like to write you words of consolation and comfort, but when you experience such a loss, words fail. The only consolation is the fact that the two boys were highly religious and must have died trusting

in God. Jean's letters spoke of his belief. From Denis, this was
well known; he lived for Christian principles.

Jean and Denis were intensely anti-German. How could they
have been otherwise? Each sincere Dutchman, that is to say
more than 90% of our people, was anti-German and was not
influenced by German propaganda. Jean and Denis felt the
duty to participate actively in the defeat of Germany, in which
we, the Dutch, continued to believe so badly ... But we were in a
bad position because the 'boches' stuck on us and undressed us
to the shirt, helped by the Dutch traitors of the NSB.

... But you will understand what happened in the hearts of your
sons. It was heroic Dutch people who gave their lives for a good
cause. For you, as their parents, the loss is painful. I sincerely
hope that with God's help you will be able to bear this pain.

De Vos wrote of Denis:

Denis has done a lot for his country; he was a brave, heroic boy
who, like so many others, fell into the hands of our executioners.
Believe me, I had a lot of affection for Denis, but I couldn't save
him from his sad fate.

Not long after the war ended, my father Charles Béliard received
a letter from my great-uncle Denis Mesritz, who also noted the
bravery of Denis:

I have just received a letter from my brother [Léo] of 28th July
replying to the documents I had sent him, with much care,
telling him about the death of both his two children.

They [Léo and Ernestine] are heartbroken, which is completely understandable. I fear that we will no longer see my brother in Holland.

His son Denis has been a hero; he started an illegal paper in Holland, with remarkable courage, he helped and supported all those, who like him, were part of the resistance ...

My brother wrote that, in spite of all their suffering, they can only be proud of the behaviour of their two boys.

In a letter to Willem Feuilletau de Bruyn dated the 27th of June 1945, a fellow prisoner of Neuengamme, **Hans van Ketwich Verschuur**, reflected on the loss of two great Dutch resistance fighters and friends, **Professor Telders** and Jean Mesritz:

With his [Jean's] great friend, Professor Telders, he stayed there, both an irreparable loss for their families, but no less for our country.

Although Telders had already proven himself for the Fatherland, so that we were sure that he would play a very great role in the construction and repair of our country, Jean's friends were convinced that he too was among those who would have a great job to do.

A month after the war ended, liberated fellow inmate of Bergen-Belsen, Jacob Asscher Jr, wrote about Jean Mesritz in a letter to **Madame Roosje Furstner**:

Finally, I can only tell you that Jean was appreciated by all as a good comrade and a valiant patriot. He courageously suffered

the terrible fate that affected us all. Let this thought at least be
a consolation for his parents.

Denis in Memoriam

Groningen University, when it was once more able to embrace
its motto 'Vivat, Crescat, Floreat Academia Groningana!' (Live,
Grow, Flourish Groningen Academy!) also offered reverent
commemoration for those university members who gave their
lives for the spiritual freedom of their homeland. A plaque
displays the names of professors, officials and alumni who died
in the resistance, or otherwise perished as victims of the Second
World War.

Figure 43: Monique Bond and brother Luc Béliard in 2013, at the wall of
honour in Groningen University. Researcher and author Ron van Hasselt
showed them around, helping them discover more about their uncles' lives.
Visual highlight added by Nicole Murray.

In their 1945 almanac (calendar of events), Groningen University honoured Denis Mesritz (translated by Dini Elting):

> Denis was a good friend, many members of Vindicat remember him as a comrade who was a great support to them in their lives. Denis was blessed with extraordinary gifts in almost every area: he has used them with a selflessness and a self-sacrifice that fills us who knew him with admiration. He was a loyal member of the Corps [Student Association] ...

> This almanac can only express the thanks that countless people in the Netherlands, who owe him much, and sometimes everything, would give to him.

> Denis was active; he did not walk only the well-trodden paths, but he always created new possibilities himself. He was one of the few, who, from the beginning, opposed National Socialism; it soon became a life or death struggle for him. His closed and somewhat stiff nature did not make it easy to understand him. Only afterwards did it really dawn on us what we have lost in him. Now that the recovery is in progress and we sometimes feel powerless, we realise that many of the best have fallen.

> It is an impossible task to list all of Denis' functions. The Groningen University community honours him as a leader of the student resistance. Having graduated, he left for the Hague; there too he was one of the leaders of illegality in nearly all areas. He did not shy away from danger. Finally, in May 1944, he was arrested in the train by the Sicherheitsdienst, initially only on account of a little error in his identity card. However, his identity soon became known.

Denis has fallen; he died in the camp at Rathenau. The Nederlandsche Christen-Studenten Vereeniging (Dutch Christian Student Society) also loses in him its general chairman: Denis had adopted Christ and had put his whole life in His service; the key to all his indefatigable work, his great humility, his gentleness of judgment, is Christ's commandment to love your neighbour as yourself. His unshakable faith has helped him through everything, right down to the end. He will continue to be a shining example for us. Denis is one of the men who laid the foundation for the New Netherlands. His whole life is a testimony that no one can lay any other foundation than that which is laid, which is Jesus Christ.

J. R. v. D. L. [Johan Reinhardt van der Leeuw]

The Cross of Resistance

On the 7th of May 1946, Denis Mesritz was named as a recipient of the newly instituted Verzetskruis, or Dutch Cross of Resistance. This decoration was awarded by Royal Decree in recognition of *exceptional courage and conduct in the resistance against the enemies of the Dutch cause, and for maintaining mental freedom.*

The citation can be translated as:

For in dangerous circumstances having shown courage, initiative, obstinacy, sacrifice and dedication in the battle against the oppressor of the Dutch independence and keeping up spiritual freedom, and so honouring in him one of the ways of resistance, that was shown in its many forms from 15th May 1940 until 5th May 1945 in growing manner inflicting

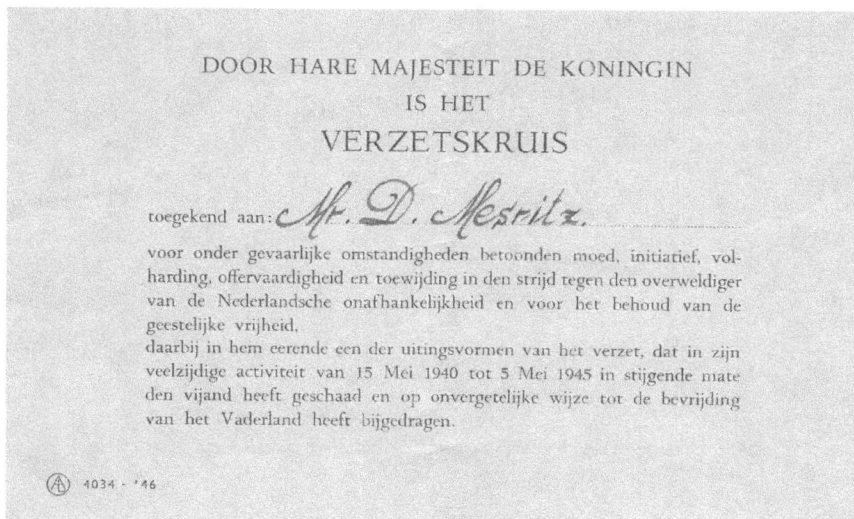

DOOR HARE MAJESTEIT DE KONINGIN
IS HET
VERZETSKRUIS

toegekend aan: *Mr. D. Mesritz.*

voor onder gevaarlijke omstandigheden betoonden moed, initiatief, volharding, offervaardigheid en toewijding in den strijd tegen den overweldiger
van de Nederlandsche onafhankelijkheid en voor het behoud van de
geestelijke vrijheid,
daarbij in hem eerende een der uitingsvormen van het verzet, dat in zijn
veelzijdige activiteit van 15 Mei 1940 tot 5 Mei 1945 in stijgende mate
den vijand heeft geschaad en op onvergetelijke wijze tot de bevrijding
van het Vaderland heeft bijgedragen.

4034 - '46

Figure 44: Denis' award citation for the Cross of Resistance.

damage to the enemies' cause and having contributed in an
unforgettable way to the liberation of the homeland.[53]

The medal is a bronze cross on a flaming star, surmounted by a crown. In the centre, Saint George (the Resistance) kills the dragon (the Nazis). The arms of the cross are inscribed TROUW TOT IN DEN DOOD (loyal unto death). The reverse shows a flaming sword severing a chain. It hangs from a crimson gallon, with an orange line at each edge.

Figure 45: The Verzetskruis, as awarded to Denis Mesritz, posthumously, in May 1946.

[53] www.tracesofwar.com/persons/34209/Mesritz-Denis-Claire-Baudouin.htm

7 Mei 1946

No. 17

Wij Wilhelmina, bij de gratie Gods,

Koningin der Nederlanden, Prinses van

Oranje-Nassau, enz., enz., enz.

Op de voordracht van Onzen Minister-
President d.d. 7 Mei 1946 No. 11196;

HEBBEN GOEDGEVONDEN EN VERSTAAN:

Toe te kennen het Verzetskruis (posthuum) aan:

Ir. H.J. van Aalderen
P. van As
J. van den Bosch
D.A. van den Bosch
J.H. Bosch
L. Bleys
M. Crans
Dr. R.J. Dam
H. Dienske
F. Duwaer
H. Gelder
W. Gertenbach
P.G.S. Guermonprez
Mr. C.H. de Groot
W. van Hall
Th.W.L. Baron van Heemstra
J. Hendriks
W.J. Henkels
J. Baron van Hövell tot Westerflier
H. Hos
A.M.L. Hesselbergs
J. van der Horst
L. Jansen
Dr. G.W. Kasteyn
A. Keuter
H.Th. Kuypers-Rietberg
A. Meerwaldt
Professor Dr.Ir. J.A.A. Mekel
Mr. D. Mesritz
L. Moonen
F. Nieuwenhuysen
B. Oosthoek

Wij Wilhelmina, bij de gratie Gods,

Koningin der Nederlanden, Prinses van

Oranje-Nassau, enz., enz., enz.

Professor Mr. J. Oranje
Tj. Pannekoek
J. Post
Professor Mr. V.H. Rutgers
W. Santema
Mejuffrouw A. Schaft
Professor Ir. R.L.A. Schoemaker
W. Speelman
Professor Mr. B.M. Telders
O.R. Thomsen
T.W. Tourton de Bruin
L.M. Valstar
G.v.d.Veen
F.M.R. Versteegh
C. Vlot
Dr. H.B. Wiardi-Beckman
J.H. Westerveld
J. Wüthrich

wegens onder gevaarlijke omstandigheden betoonden moed,
initiatief, volharding, offervaardigheid en toewijding in
den strijd tegen den overweldiger van de Nederlandsche onafhankelijkheid en voor het behoud van de geestelijke vrijheid,
daarbij in hen eerende de verschillende uitingsvormen van het
verzet, dat in zijn veelzijdige activiteit van 15 Mei 1940
tot 5 Mei 1945 in stijgende mate den vijand heeft geschaad
en op onvergetelijke wijze tot de bevrijding van het vaderland heeft bijgedragen.

Onze Minister-President is belast met de
uitvoering van dit Besluit.

Het dorp, den 7 Mei 1946.

De Minister-President,

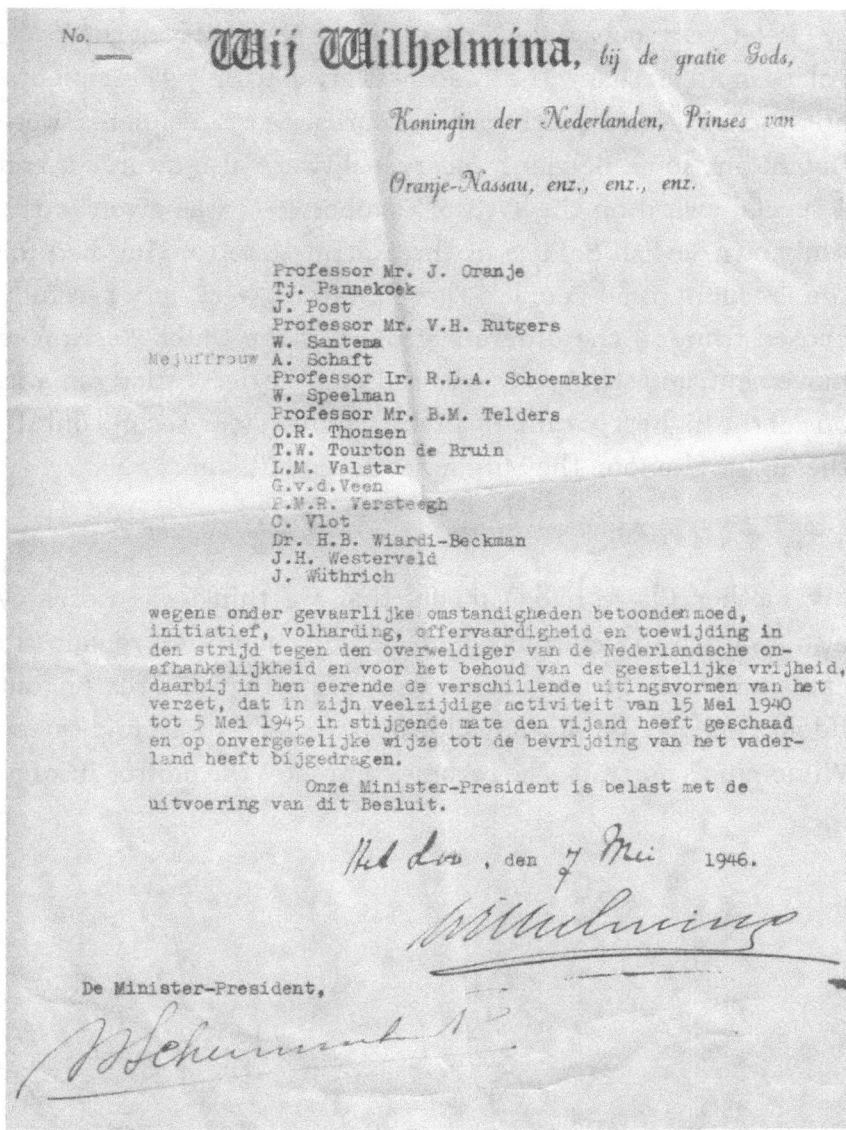

Figure 46: Royal decree 17, dated 7 May 1946, listing those awarded the 95 Dutch Crosses of Resistance.

Relatives received the crosses on the 9th of May at the Royal Palace in Amsterdam. The award was given to only 95 recipients, of which 93 were posthumous awards. Most recipients were Dutch, but some Belgians and French were also awarded, and a special award on the 17th of October 1947 was given to the 'Unknown Jewish Soldier of the Warsaw Ghetto who died for the Freedom of all People'. Those awarded were very carefully chosen from all the different groups of the Dutch Resistance movement, and strict rules ensured that the decoration remains one of the highest in ranking in the Dutch system, second only to the highest honour, the Military Order of William.

The WWII De Geuzen Medal

My mother Claire had a medal that we think was probably also awarded to Denis, although no documentation remains to explain it. It is a Geuzen medal, inscribed with the words 'En tout fidelles au roy' (In all things loyal to the Queen) around Queen Wilhemina's portrait. The reverse completes the motto: 'jusques

Figure 47: WWII Geuzen medal, most likely awarded to Denis.

à porter la besase' (even if it means carrying the beggar's pouch) around clasped hands with the dates 1942 and 1945, and the number 9.

I have only a superficial understanding of the cultural significance of the De Geuzen in the Netherlands, which dates back to the late 1500s. Could the medal have signified membership of the 'De Geuzen' resistance group? Did the figure 9 denote Denis' membership of the Council of Nine? I imagine that this medal symbolises fierce loyalty to the independence of the Netherlands.

Legacy of Bravery

Tributes to both Jean and Denis Mesritz continued for decades after their deaths. In 1992, Supreme Court Justice and Leiden University lecturer **Huib Drion** spoke of his article, 'The romantic roots of democracy', written in April 1944 as an elaboration of a lecture he had given to an audience in the Hague. He had wanted to address the elitist thinking that was popular in many circles in the 1930s. Drion dedicated his observations to his friend, resistance fighter Denis Mesritz:

> *Mesritz was a first-rate man who dedicated himself completely in his underground work. Unfortunately, in the last year of the war he was arrested in the train just after he left our house, and furthermore then it was discovered that he was 'half-Jewish'. He didn't survive. A rare, incorruptible and sensitive man who made an enormous contribution to the Resistance.*

Lamenting the loss of **Lodo van Hamel** and Jean Mesritz, **Erik Michielsen** wrote in his memoir, *Against the Blows of the Eastern Wind*:

It would be good to talk about what could have been if they were successful. It would have been a well-remembered event considering what they were up against. Lodo and Jean wouldn't have died in the conditions they did.

In September 2009, during a radio interview for *Het Parool*, Louis Tas (also known as Loden Vogel), psychiatrist and concentration camp survivor, was asked:

No matter how successful your life has been, you must have suffered losses?

In his reply, Tas singled out the death of Jean Mesritz:

Because of the war you lose a few years; I could have started earlier doing useful work. And then, of course, [there are] the valuable and kind people who died at a young age. For example, Jean Mesritz, a fine fellow who I met in Westerbork. He was caught trying to set out to sea with a row boat near Scheveningen. Death, that is the real loss.

Another lovely tribute came in January 2014 when our friend Ron van Hasselt told us this story from Mrs Han Leutscher (née Hazelhoff). She said that her cousin, Adolf 'Attie' Hazelhoff-Heeres had been friends with Denis Mesritz. Attie was interned in a death cell during the war, but survived. Attie had told her that if he ever had a son he would call him Denis, after his friend Denis Mesritz.

Today an organisation called Oorlogsgravenstichting cares for Dutch War graves. On the eve of the 5th of May each year, a silent walk takes place so that civilians can remember the courage and humanity of those lost.

Jean and Denis are listed together on the Honour Roll of the Fallen (1940–1945), which is kept in the entrance hall of the Dutch House of Representatives. Each day one page is turned, to reveal new names to the public. The roll lists the names of those who gave their lives as soldiers or resistance fighters for the Kingdom of the Netherlands in the Second World War.[54]

Mesritz

Jean Adrien Claire
's-Gravenhage   2 · III · 1918
Student
Hannover   15 · III · 1945

Mesritz

Denis Claire Baudouin
's-Gravenhage   16 · X · 1919
Jurist
Rathenau   16 · III · 1945

Figure 48: Entries for Jean and Denis on the Honour Roll of the Fallen. Note the dates here, which do not quite match those from other sources.

---

[54] To accommodate edits and additions, the Roll of Honor has also been digitised at www.erelijst.nl. You can search for Jean and Denis, and put a flower next to their names.

Afterword

In writing this book, I have learnt something about what it was like to live through the war in the Netherlands, and something of the lives and deaths of my Dutch uncles, Jean and Denis Mesritz. I have the impression that, before the war at least, the Dutch considered themselves to be superior to everyone. It seems that both of the brothers hated the Germans and referred to them as stupid! The Dutch were amongst the richest people in the world, particularly those who attended Leiden University, as the Mesritz family and their contemporaries did, and they believed that they were worthy of it. I don't really know whether the war shook this belief.

My grandparents, Léo and Ernestine, were churchgoers and, while Denis was very much a believer too, it seems that religion was less important to Jean. Both young men probably also sought adventure. The war was a terrible thing, but these were young men in the prime of their life. Just think how exciting it would have been for Jean at the age of 21, preparing to make a daring escape to England, with the prospect of becoming a fighter pilot to foil the Nazis! Perhaps Jean was lured by the idea of doing something dangerous, as well as helping to save the Dutch people.

From what I've read and heard, it's clear that my uncle Jean cared for people, and he also enjoyed working with horses in the army, and was very fond of his dog. Close friend, author, and feted 'Soldier of Orange' **Erik Hazelhoff** admired Jean a lot, and we were sorry to find out that we missed meeting

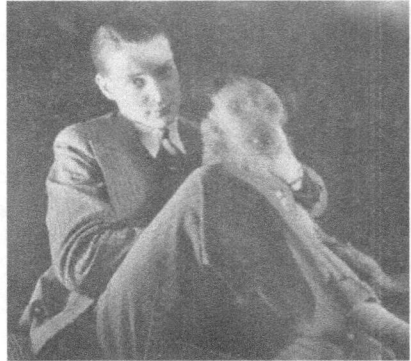

Figure 49: Jean Mesritz with his beloved dog.

Erik by mere months when he passed away a few years ago. Jean was someone who, if things needed to happen, stepped up to do them. In prison, it seems he found an inner strength that helped many people. He was attractive and charismatic, and he used these characteristics to ease many of his fellow inmates' time in prison. This is such a different kind of strength to that required for daring undertakings — yet no less valuable.

Figure 50: Denis travelled widely in his work for the resistance.

As for my uncle Denis, according to Jos de Vos, he made a huge contribution to the resistance effort. He was the kind of person who helped people, who went out no matter the weather, who organised things: coordinating resistance efforts and publishing illegal papers. De Vos believed that there were hundreds of people who owed Denis enormously. What De Vos says about Denis runs deep, and he put a lot of time and care into his letters concerning him. I really wish that some of Denis' writing had survived so that we could have a deeper understanding of what inspired this young man.

It was a tragedy for their family that both my uncles died, and awful to think that they were so close to surviving the war. I also find it terribly sad that they were not able to support each other in their resistance efforts — once Jean had been imprisoned in October 1940, we know of only one time that their paths crossed before they died, at Vught camp in the second half of 1944, and we don't know whether they were able to share more than a few moments with each other.

One more story shows how the war could take people down unexpected paths: this is the tale of a student friend of Jean and Erik Hazelhoff, Alexander Rowerth. Alexander had enlisted in the Dutch Army before the war broke out. Once war was declared, however, his parents — who were Dutch but of German origin — were taken into custody by the Dutch and held in prison. In *Soldier of Orange*, Hazelhoff relates how, a couple of days later, Alexander rang and asked if he would come and visit, particularly as Alexander's mother was not handling the situation well. But Erik did not want to visit people who were suspected of being collaborators. The next time the Leideners saw Alexander, he was

Figure 51: Ernestine and Léo Mesritz at daughter Claire's home, Witherenden Mill in Sussex, England, about 10 or 15 years after the end of WWII.

in German uniform. At the end of the war, however, Hazelhoff wrote that he received a postcard from Alexander from Russia that read: *Sorry guys, but we're still friends, aren't we?* Alexander later died fighting with the SS in the Ukraine.

After the war, my grandparents Léo and Ernestine returned to Europe and their house in Eze, France. Léo soon visited Holland, found *Lize*, and organised a lifelong stipend for her, in thanks for her care and support of both Jean and Denis throughout the war. After that visit, however, my grandparents refused to go to the Netherlands ever again. In their old age they moved to Switzerland.

My mother, who had divorced my father when I was only two years old, married an Englishman with strong ties to Italy. Claire and Charles Nalder had two daughters together, my younger sisters Annie and Alex. My older siblings remained in France, and I lived with Claire and her new family in England and then at Lake Como in Italy. It is to Annie that our mother gave the Geuzen medal. In the mid-1950s, I was finally able to reconnect with my father, and I visited him regularly in France until his death on the 17th of August 1967.

Both Léo and Ernestine died in Switzerland: Léo in 1965 and Ernestine in 1968. I remember visiting them there on the way home from Oxford University to my mother and step-father's house near Castellina in Chianti, Italy in the early 1960s. They were, as always, pleased to see me and good to talk to, but the lives and sacrifices of Jean and Denis were never spoken of. I was

Figure 52: Claire's children — we are all family now. Upper: Mummy, Annie and me, at home at Witherenden Mill, about 1950. Middle: With my older siblings, Luc and Miki (Marie Claire) in Morocco, in about 1955. Lower: Crossing the Channel with Mummy, Alexe and Annie, about 1958.

able to visit them with my first baby, Denise, so they knew that Denis' name lived on in her.

I think I can understand that it may have been too painful for my grandparents — and even my mother — to talk about the boys they'd lost. But I find it very sad that knowledge of my uncles Lucien, Jean and Denis was effectively lost to my generation of their family.

In 1946, someone — Willem Feuilletau de Bruyn, we believe — attended the ceremony at which Denis was posthumously awarded the Cross of Resistance. Since that event, as far as I've been able to find out, no family members have been present at any of the numerous events held to commemorate the contributions made to the Dutch resistance by my uncles and their brave compatriots. I am glad to have found out something about them and to discover that their efforts were recognised and are still commemorated in the Netherlands. They are a potent reminder that the power to resist evil lies in all of us.

I hope this book reclaims their lives for our family, celebrating their strength, service, and sacrifice by keeping the memory of Jean and Denis Mesritz alive.

Key People

Names are alphabetised in the Dutch manner, discounting the prefixes de, van, van den, van 't, and vas. To assist English-speakers, the part of the name alphabetised is underlined.

Professor Lourens Gerhard Marinus <u>Baas Becking</u> (4 Jan 1895 – 6 Jan 1963) A microbiologist and professor of botany at Leiden University, Baas Becking was helping the group trying to cross to England and was arrested with Jean at Lake Tjeuke. He was acquitted and released in June 1941.

After World War II, Baas Becking became a colonel in the Red Cross, then moved to New Caledonia as president of the scientific council of the South Pacific Commission, and finally to Australia, where he continued his scientific work.

<u>Boissevain</u> family The whole family worked hard in the resistance in a variety of ways. Jan, his wife Mies, and their three sons hosted the CS6 group, whose activities included armed responses to the German occupation.

- ***Jan (Canada) Boissevain*** (14 May 1895 – 30 Jan 1945) was the first to be imprisoned, and died in Buchenwald camp.
- ***Jan-Karel (Janka) Boissevain*** (1920 – 1 Oct 1943) and ***Gideon (Gi) Boissevain*** (1921 – 1 Oct 1943). In the summer

of 1940, the brothers tried to cross to England in a boat made of wine barrels, but were arrested. They persuaded the 'Moffen' it was just a student prank, and were freed to continue their resistance work. After CS6 was betrayed in August 1943, Jan-Karel and Gideon were shot by the Nazis at Overveen.

- *Adrienne Minette (Mies) Boissevain-van Lennep* (1896–1965), and their youngest son, *Frans Boissevain* (1922–1981) focused on rescuing many Jewish children and families. Arrested by the Gestapo along with Janka and Gi, Mies and Frans were sent into the camp system, which they barely survived.

Iman Jacob Pieter van den Bosch (30 May 1891 – 28 Oct 1944) A key Dutch resistance leader and close colleague of Denis Mesritz, Van den Bosch was involved in Dutch espionage and the Council of Nine. On 18 October 1944, Van den Bosch met delegates from the various Dutch resistance organisations at a house on the Parklaan in Groningen. They were betrayed: the Germans were aware of the meeting and were waiting for the participants. Van den Bosch was hit by gunshot in the chest, and fled to a bicycle shop where he was able to get rid of incriminating papers. The SiPo followed and arrested him, but thanks to his quick actions, they did not realise that Van den Bosch was a leader of the resistance. They knew only his alias, Van den Berg — as Van den Bosch carried an identity card in his true name, no connection was made. Nonetheless, he was executed at Westerbork ten days later; his body was cremated and the ash collected in an urn by a Jewish camp occupant. On 2nd November 1945, the urn was placed in the Resistance Monument at Esserveld General Cemetery in Groningen.

Dr Willem Karel Hendrik Feuilletau de <u>Bruyn</u> (11 Jul 1886 – 13 May 1972) A soldier and researcher who led many expeditions in Seram (now part of Indonesia) and New Guinea and was politically active after WWII. He married Henriëtte Emma Mulder, niece of Madame Mulder (Jean and Denis' grandmother). Feuilletau de Bruyn and his wife were the family representatives who placed a notice of Jean and Denis' deaths in *Het Parool* in 1945.

Jan <u>Campert</u> (15 Aug 1902 – 12 Jan 1943) A journalist, theatre critic, and writer who lived in Amsterdam. Campert was arrested for aiding Jews, and died in Neuengamme concentration camp.

Professor Rudolph Pabus <u>Cleveringa</u> (2 Apr 1894 – 15 Dec 1980) Professor of Law at Leiden University, Cleveringa gave a powerful speech against the dismissal of his Jewish colleagues at student protests on the 26th of November 1940. He was arrested the next day and sent to the Oranjehotel, where he was held until 28th June 1941. He and his colleagues at Leiden University continued their resistance activities, joining the 'College van Vertouwensmannen' (College of Trusted Men). Cleveringa was re-arrested in the spring of 1944 and imprisoned in Vught. In both camps, he met up with his former student, Jean Mesritz. In his book, *Gedenkschriften*, Cleveringa wrote about Jean being a great help while they were together in Vught. He returned to university work after the war, and died just over thirty years later, aged 86.

Drion **brothers** Both Jan and Huib worked in the illegal publications that were so essential to the Dutch resistance.

- **FJW (Jan) Drion** (30 Dec 1915 – 1 Mar 1964) became one of the designers of the new Dutch civil code, and a professor at Leiden University after the war, succeeding Meijers, whose dismissal as a Jew was one of the sparks for the university strike and Cleveringa's 1940 lecture.
- **Huibert (Huib) Drion** (25 Apr 1917 – 20 Apr 2004) After WWII, Huib rose to become Supreme Court Justice, internationally known for championing euthanasia.

Kees van _Eendenburg_ (29 Dec 1914 – 2 Sep 1966). One of the three Leideners who successfully crossed from the Netherlands to England by sea in July 1940. Van Eendenburg later became part of the 322nd Dutch Squadron RAF. He was shot down near Lille, but made a belly landing and escaped the Germans. He was promoted to Squadron Leader on 12th September 1944. He retired soon after the war.

Willem (Wim) _Eggink_ (3 May 1920 – 24 Apr 1945) An Utrecht student and a leader of _Ons Volk_, Eggink worked closely with Denis Mesritz and Han Gelder. Eggink was arrested as a staff member of _Het Parool_ in early 1944. His trial took place from 25th July to 8th August 1944, during which time he married Leiden law student and _Ons Volk_ employee Johanna van Hellenberg Hubar. Eggink was held at Kamp Amersfoort until August 1944, then at Hamelin Prison, where he died just before his 25th birthday.

Madame Roosje van Lelyveld _Furstner_ (1896 – 1976) Roosje was the wife of **Dr Willem Furstner**, the Mesritz family doctor in the Hague. They were good friends of the Mesritz family and knew Jean and Denis from childhood. Jean was like a second son to Madame Furstner: she took him care packages while he was in Kamp Vught in 1943, and exchanged letters with Jacob Asscher Jr about Jean during the war.

Gustaaf Henri (Han) <u>Gelder</u> (8 Jul 1919 – 21 Jan 1944) A Leiden University student, who helped to coordinate the Dutch fight for freedom as a foreman of the Council of Nine. After helping to publish many illegal papers, Han Gelder was taken by the SiPo on 21st January 1944, during a raid on the *Het Parool* premises. Gelder bravely shot himself, so that he could not be arrested by the Nazis and risk passing on important intelligence. His sacrifice also preserved his anonymity, as he was not carrying identity papers. Gelder was awarded a Cross of Resistance, and is now buried in the Dutch Field of Honour at Loenen.

Walraven (Wally) van <u>Hall</u> (10 Feb 1906 – 12 Feb 1945) Well-known Dutch resistance leader, financier, and founder of the Resistance Bank. Van Hall was captured and executed by the Nazis in February 1945.

He was posthumously awarded the Dutch Cross of Resistance (Verzetskruis). The United States awarded him the Medal of Freedom with Gold Palm, Israel recognised him as 'Righteous Among the Nations' in 1978 for supporting and funding between 800 and 900 Jews in hiding during the war. In honour of his deeds in the resistance, in 2010 a monument was erected near the office of the Dutch Central Bank, at the Frederiksplein 40 in Amsterdam.

Lieutenant-Commander Lodewijk Anne Rinze Jetse (Lodo) van Hamel (6 Jun 1915 – 16 Jun 1941), was a Dutch naval officer (Lieutenant Commander second class) at the Fort in IJmuiden at the outbreak of World War II in the Netherlands. He helped evacuate the British Army from Dunkirk as Commander of Hr. Ms. motorboat *M74* before becoming the first Dutch secret agent in the occupied Netherlands (alias Willem van Dalen). Van Hamel was a childhood friend of the Mesritz family, and he was arrested at Lake Tjeuke with Jean Mesritz and executed by order of a German military court. Van Hamel's resistance work was continued by his older brother Gerard van Hamel (1911 – 1944). Posthumous awards for Lodo van Hamel include the Military Order of William (Knight 4th Class) and the Resistance Commemoration Cross.

Siebren (Erik Hazelhoff) Roelfzema (3 Apr 1917 – 26 Sep 2007) An important figure in the Dutch resistance, RAF fighter pilot Hazelhoff was a very close friend of Jean Mesritz, and undertook many undercover missions for the Dutch government-in-exile.

Near the end of the war, Hazelhoff was appointed Adjutant (assistant) to Queen Wilhelmina. He was awarded the RAF Distinguished Flying Cross and made a Knight 4th Class of the Military William Order. Hazelhoff was also a writer, and his memoir, *Soldier of Orange*, has been made into a film and a stage musical.

Doctor Johannes Floris Philippus (Hans) Hers (4 Jul 1917 – 29 Oct 2006) Hers was arrested with his friend Jean Mesritz at Lake Tjeuke. After serving a three-year sentence, during which he married Toos Schreuder, Hers was kept in 'Schutzhaft' (a kind of protective custody) until the end of the war, at Münster prison, Brual-Rhede camp, Waldheim prison, and Zwickau prison. He was moved to Sachsenhausen camp on 29th July 1944, where he was a doctor in the infirmary. When Russian and Polish soldiers liberated the camp on 22nd April 1945, Hers stayed with the sick, and did not return to the Netherlands until 11th August 1945. After the war, Hers had to start his medical studies in Leiden again, because exam results from before the war were no longer valid. He obtained his doctorate cum laude in November 1954. In 1985, Hans Hers was awarded the Grand Cross of Honour in the House Order of Orange.

Jozef Felix Henri Marie Baron van <u>Hövell</u> van Wezeveld en Westerflier (Jos van Hövell) (12 Jan 1919 – 3 Jan 1945) A founding member of the Council of Nine and close friend of Denis Mesritz. Denis stayed with Van Hövell for a time during the war. On the night of 27th March 1944, Jos van Hövell was arrested in the Hague, held in the Oranjehotel for 3 months, and then moved to the Herzogenbusch concentration camp (Kamp Vught). In September 1944 he was deported via Sachsenhausen to Neuengamme concentration camp, where he had to do heavy forced labour. He died of exhaustion on 13th January 1945, at the age of 25. He was posthumously awarded the Dutch Cross of Resistance (Verzetskruis).

Henricus Petrus Johannes (Hans) van <u>Ketwich Verschuur</u> (11 Jan 1905 – 1996) was held in Vught, Amersfoort and Neuengamme camps from 1942 to 1945. In May 1945, he survived a torpedo attack on the transport ship Cap Arona (in Lubeck), before becoming Director-General of the Dutch Red Cross (1946–51). He was later appointed as Envoy to the Red Cross in Lebanon from 1951–1952.

Carel Henrik (Cally) _Kranenburg_ (25 Aug 1917 – 17 Mar 1947) Following officer training at Amersfoort, Carel served in the Royal Netherlands Army. Kranenburg was a friend of Jean Mesritz, codenamed 'The Hussar', and he was one of the group arrested at Lake Tjeuke, but he was released on 16 April 1941. On 29 July 1945, Kranenburg was seconded to the Marine Corps. He trained further in Scotland and the United States and on 17 November left for the East Indies on secondment to the Navy, arriving in Java on 10th March 1946. On 17th March 1947, his armoured car was attacked, and he was killed when he opened the turret's valve to shoot his attacker. Kranenburg was reburied in the Dutch Field of Honour, Kembang Kuning, in Surabaya.

Helena _Kuipers-Rietberg_ (codename Tante Riek) (26 May 1893 – 27 Dec 1944) Founder of the Landelijke Organisatie Voor Hulp Aan Onderduikers (LO), the National Organisation for Help to People in Hiding, which operated between mid-1942 and May 1945, and saved the lives of thousands of people. Before WWII, Madame Kuipers-Rietberg had been active in creating a national organisation of Dutch women of the Reformed church, which was helpful in forming the LO's networks. She and her husband, Piet, had five children.

When they were captured in May 1944, the couple agreed that Helena would take full responsibility for the actions of the LO, in the hope that reprisals against a woman would be less severe. She was sent to Vught and then Ravensbruck, where she died on the 27 of December 1944. Piet and their five children survived the war.

Lize Jean and Denis' childhood nanny, and later housekeeper at Madame Mulder's house, Lize was dedicated in her support of the family. She visited Jean in Kamp Vught, taking him care parcels, and lied, at considerable risk to herself, about recognising Denis. Léo returned to the Hague after the war and provided Lize a lifelong stipend in gratitude for her care of his mother and sons. The fact that Lize is one of the few people for whom we have not been able to find a surname is probably a reflection of the social stratification in Dutch society at that time and does not represent any lack of respect on my part for this brave and caring woman.

Arthur Meerwaldt (23 Oct 1918 – 8 Jan 1945) An editor and publisher who worked closely with Denis Mesritz to produce *Ons Volk* and the resistance papers *Bron*, *De Geus* and *Het Parool*.

Following his arrest by the Nazis, on 25th May 1944, Meerwaldt was transferred to Amersfoort transit camp, then Wolvenplein prison in Utrecht. At his trial in July–August 1944 in Utrecht, although the death penalty was demanded for prisoners of the *Het Parool* Group, he was instead sentenced to fifteen years in prison. He was transferred to Hamelin prison, and eventually to Eschershausen labour camp, where, weakened by hunger, cold and neglect, he died of pneumonia on 8 January 1945. Meerwaldt is now buried at the Dutch Field of Honour near Hannover.

Michielsen brothers Both Erik and Karel were 'Den Haag' youngsters, and later part of the Leidener set. They escaped separately to England, where they continued to serve the Dutch resistance.

- **Erik Frits Karel Michielsen** (8 Jul 1916 – 26 Aug 1944) Erik Michielsen was a good friend of Jean Mesritz, and a Reserve Lieutenant of the Dutch Field Artillery, who fought in the Battle of Grebbeberg (10 May 1940). He reached England in June 1942, after six failed attempts, and joined the air force, dying in August 1944 during 'Bullseye' night flying training in Shropshire. He was just twenty-eight years old. Erik's memoir, *Against the Gusts of the East Wind,* was published posthumously in 1945.
- **Karel Michielsen** (1918 – 1996) One of the three Leideners who successfully crossed from the Netherlands to England by sea, in July 1940, in Van Eendenburg's *Bebek.* Michielsen, a close friend of Jean Mesritz, survived the war. His memoir, *Bygone Glory,* remains unpublished.

Alfred David (Fred) vas Nunes (3 Sep 1914 – 16 Jan 2008) One of the three Leideners who successfully crossed from the Netherlands to England by sea, in July 1940. A lawyer, after the war, Vas Nunes became embassy consul at the United Nations in New York and Director of Shell Nederland.

Bob Oosthoek (25 Jun 1912 – 12 Oct 1944) An actor and drama teacher in the Hague who also worked with the LO, and collaborated with financier Van Hall. He was a key member of the Council of Nine and distributed the illegal journals *De Stem van Strijdend Nederland* and *Ons Volk.* Oosthoek was arrested on 22nd August 1944, and subjected to such severe torture at the Oranjehotel that he was partially paralysed. His body was found on the railway tracks on the way to Kamp Neuengamme. He was posthumously awarded the Dutch Cross of Resistance (Verzetskruis).

François van 't Sant (11 Feb 1883 – 3 Jun 1966) Working closely with Queen Wilhelmina throughout WWII, as he had done in WWI and the inter-war years, Van 't Sant became head of the Dutch secret intelligence service in exile in London during the war. He became a controversial figure, with many considering him to have too much influence with the Queen, and too much power. Van 't Sant continued to serve the House of Orange-Nassau after the war.

Marion Smit It seems most likely that Marion Smit was Van Hamel's girlfriend. Part of Jean Mesritz's group trying to cross to England, Smit was arrested in Oct 1940, convicted, but then acquitted and released in June 1941. The German trial notes suggest that Smit had organised safe houses for Van Hamel, and that Van Hamel had promised to take both his loved one (Smit) and Jean Mesritz with him to England.

Professor Benjamin Marius Telders (19 Mar 1903 – 6 Apr 1945) The son of lawyer and attorney Wilhelm Albert Telders; a Dutch lawyer, politician (Liberal State Party chairman), and professor of international law at Leiden University.

Telders was heavily involved with the Dutch resistance, along with Prof. Cleveringa. He published illegal papers and mobilised students in protest, which led to his arrest on 18th

December 1940. He was held in at least five different camps — Scheveningen, Buchenwald, Vught, Sachsenhausen, and Bergen-Belsen, where he died just nine days before liberation. Telders was posthumously awarded the Cross of Resistance.

Antonius Franciscus (Anton) van <u>Velsen</u> (17 Nov 1917 – Sep 1995) Appointed Second Lieutenant of the Marines just a few weeks before the Nazi invasion of the Netherlands, Van Velsen was arrested for espionage in 1941 and imprisoned in Sachsenhausen concentration camp, then moved via Auschwitz-Buna to Birkenau in December 1942. After the war, Van Velsen saw active service in the East Indies, and lost his left leg. After his retirement from the military, he became a lawyer. In Frankfurt, in 1964, he testified at a war crimes trial of Auschwitz personnel.

Jacob (Jos) de <u>Vos</u> A close friend and advisor of Léo, Jean, and Denis Mesritz. Denis lived for a period during WWII at De Vos' offices in the Hague. During and after the war, De Vos wrote several detailed letters to those who asked after Jean, or Denis, or both.

References

published works, sorted by author

Biderman, Abraham H. *The World of My Past*. AHB Publications, 1995.

Calis, Piet. De vrienden van weleer. Schrijvers en tijdschriften tussen 1945 en 1948 [The Friends of Yesteryear: Writers and Magazines between 1945 and 1948]. Meulenhoff, 1999. www.dbnl.org/tekst/cali002vrie01_01, viewed 21 May 2021.

Campert, Jan. 'The Song of the Eighteen Dead'. Translated by E Prins and CM MacInnes in *War Poetry from Occupied Holland*. Arrowsmith, 1945. www.echenberg.org/war-poetry.com_oldsite/_data/conflicts/details/62618.html, and stfillanschurch.org.uk/wp-content/uploads/2020/04/The-Song-of-the-Eighteen-Dead-040520.pdf, viewed 30 Apr 2021.

Cleveringa, RP. *Gedenkschriften. Betreffende zijn gevangenschap in 1940–1941 en 1944 [Memoirs of imprisonment in 1940–41 and 1944]*. EJ Brill University Press, Leiden, 1983. Translated from the German edition by Tineke Schoonens.

Drion, Huib. 'The romantic roots of democracy'. Paper. The Hague, April 1944.

van Hasselt, R. De oorlog van mijn vader [My father's war]. Profiel, Bedum, 2012.

—— Uitgesloten, [Excluded]. Aspekt, Soesterberg, in press.

Hazelhoff, Erik. *Soldier of Orange*. Hodder and Stoughton, 1972.

Herber, Rob. *Nico Bloembergen: Master of Light*. Springer International, 2019.

Ignatieff, M. 'Civil Courage and the Moral Imagination: Cleveringa Lecture given by Prof. Dr. Michael Ignatieff'. Leiden University, 26 Nov 2013.

Kolb, Eberhard. *Bergen-Belsen: From 1943 to 1945*, 2nd edn. Sammlunb Vandenhoeck, 1988.

Koker, David. *At the Edge of the Abyss: A Concentration Camp Diary 1943-1944*. Northwestern University Press, 2012.

Lalor, Ailish. 'The Hunger Winter: the Dutch famine of 1944-45', *Dutch Review*, 1 May 2021, dutchreview.com/culture/the-hunger-winter-the-dutch-famine-of-1944-45, viewed 4 Mar 2021.

Marlin, John Tepper, 2015, *WW2 | 6. Armed Resistance: Jan Canada and Sons (Updated Feb. 9, 2016)* https://cityeconomist.blogspot.com/2015/01/active-resistance-to-nazis-jan-canada.html

Michielsen, Erik. *Tegen de vlagen van den Oostenwind [Against the Gusts of the Eastern Wind]*. Leiden, 1945.

O'Connor, Bernard. *Bletchley Park and the Pigeon Spies* (ebook). Lulu.com, 2018. pp. 56–57.

Rep, Jelte. *Englandspeil, Spionagetragedie in bezet Nederland 1942-1944* [The English Game: Espionage Tragedy in the Occupied Netherlands 1942–1944]. Van Holkema & Warendorf, 1977.

Schulten, CM. *Zeg mij aan wien ik toebehoor [Tell me to whom I belong]*. Rijksinstituut voor Oorlogsdocumentatie, 1993. Translated by Tineke Schoonens.

Tas, Louis, alias Loden Vogel (1920–2011). *Dagboek uit een kamp [Diary from a Camp]*. 1946, consulted via DBNL. www.dbnl.org/tekst/voge006dagb01_01/index.php, viewed 1 Feb 2022.

—— 'Mijn wijsheid is een ziekteverschijnsel' [My Wisdom is a Disease Symptom], *Het Parool*. 1 October, 2009. www.parool.nl/nieuws/mijn-wijsheid-is-een-ziekteverschijnsel~b65b48fe, viewed 21 Apr 2021.

Vereniging van Groningse Oud-Illegale Werkers [Association of Groningen Former Illegal Workers]. Hoe Groningen Streed: provinciaal gedenkboek van het verzet 1940–1945 *[How Groningen Fought: provincial memorial book of the resistance 1940–1945]*. J Niemeijer, 1949, pp 166–188. Translated by Tineke Schoonens.

Winkel, Lydia. *De Ondergrondse Pers 1940-1945 [The Underground Press 1940-1945]*. Rijkinstituut voor Oorlogsdocumentatie, 3rd edn 1989, p. 181. http://publications.niod.knaw.nl/publications/WinkelDeVries_OndergrondsePers_1940-1945.pdf, viewed 26 Jan 2022.

published works, sorted by article or website title

'Aircrew remembered: loss of Erik Michielsen', http://aircrewremembered.com/1944-08-26-loss-of-erik-michielsen, viewed 4 Mar 2021.

'Aryan Declaration', www.meeroverdeholocaust.nl/en-glossary/aryan-declaration, viewed 7 Apr 2021.

Biografisch Woordenboek van Nederland 1880–2000. *[Biographical Dictionary of the Netherlands 1880–2000]*. Huygens ING, 1989. resources.huygens.knaw.nl/bwn1880-2000

- 'Neher, Lambertus (1889–1967)' by JG Visser, resources. huygens.knaw.nl/bwn1880-2000/lemmata/bwn1/neher, viewed 1 Feb 2022
- 'Telders, Benjamin Marius (1903–1945)' by I Schöffer, resources.huygens.knaw.nl/bwn1880-2000/BWN/ lemmata/bwn3/telders, viewed 2 Sep 2021.

'Camp Westerbork transport schedules', http://www.holocaust-lestweforget.com/westerbork-transport-schedule.html, viewed 1 Feb 2022.

Digitaal Monument 'Jean Claire Adrien Mesritz' monument. vriendenkringneuengamme.nl/person/403267/jean-claire-adrien-mesritz

'Determined Dutchmen', https://www.key.aero/article/ determined-dutchmen, viewed 1 Feb 2022.

'The Dutch Resistance Movement (Current Intelligence Study no. 6)'. www.cia.gov/readingroom/docs/DOC_0000709432. pdf, viewed 1 Feb 2022.

Europe Remembers articles: europeremembers.com

- 'The Hague in World War Two', europeremembers.com/ story/the-hague-in-world-war-two, viewed 21 May 2021
- 'The Oranjehotel' europeremembers.com/destination/ the-oranjehotel, viewed 1 Feb 2022.

Encyclopaedia Britannica online entries: www.britannica.com
- 'Night and Fog Decree', viewed 22 Oct, 2021
- 'Fifth column', viewed 9 Dec 2020

Go Dutch articles: www.godutch.com
- 'Veterans "Prinses Irene Brigade" help celebrate unit's 60th anniversary', www.godutch.com/newspaper/index. php?id=316, viewed 27 Jan 2022
- 'Germans gradually turned screws on occupied country (1931–1944): Chronology of Dutch war-time history', www. godutch.com/newspaper/index.php?id=295, viewed 7 Apr 2021.

'The Hague advised to offer $2.75 million in Holocaust restitution'. *The Times of Israel*, 1 March 2017, www.timesofisrael.com/ the-hague-advised-to-offer-2-75-million-in-holocaust- restitution, viewed 26 Jan 2021.

Holocaust Encyclopedia, United States Holocaust Memorial Museum, https://encyclopedia.ushmm.org/content/en/ article/the-netherlands, viewed 1 Feb 2022.

[Lucien Mesritz death notice], *Algemeen Handelsblad* [newspaper], 11 Jun 1935. p. 8. https://www.delpher.nl/nl/kranten, viewed 21 May 2021.

'Mesritz Jean Claire Adrien', Extract from the Registry of Military Personnel from the Royal Netherlands Marine, Army, Air Force and Military Police.

Nieuwe Rotterdamsche Courant, VG IV, 301-309 and 318-324, June 1940.

NIOD collection

- Hers, JFPh. 'Statement made on October 15, 1945'
- Wiltens, AJ Andrée. 'Statement of Wiltens made on November 3, 1947'
- 'Honorary List Category: Resistance Origin: E in de: 6994', [information pertaining to the arrest of Denis Mesritz] 16 May 1944.

'OD: Ordedienst', www.cryptomuseum.com/intel/od/index. htm, viewed 1 Feb 2022.

'Oorlogsgravenstichting' [War Graves Foundation]

- Denis Claire Baudouin Mesritz', oorlogsgravenstichting. nl/personen/102232/denis-claire-baudouin-mesritz, viewed 4 Mar 2021
- 'Jean Claire Adrien Mesritz' oorlogsgravenstichting.nl/ personen/102250/jean-claire-adrien-mesritz, viewed 20 Feb 2022.

Traces Of War articles: www.tracesofwar.com

- 'Mesritz, Denis Claire Baudouin', viewed 12 Apr 2022
- 'Misburg Hannover Concentration Camp', viewed 21 May 2021
- 'Raid on the Population Registry of Amsterdam', viewed 2 Feb 2022
- 'Verzetskruis 1940–1945 (VKN)', viewed 31 Mar 2021.

Wikipedia articles (English edition): en.wikipedia.org/wiki

- 'Abraham Asscher', viewed 1 Feb 2021
- 'Battle of Britain', viewed 2 Feb 2022
- 'Benjamin Marius Telders', viewed 4 Mar 2021

- 'Dirk Jan de Geer', viewed 7 Apr 2021
- 'Dutch-Paris', viewed 3 Feb 2021
- 'Dutch resistance', viewed 13 Apr 2021
- 'Dutch Cross of Resistance', viewed 31 Mar 2021
- 'German invasion of Belgium (1940)', viewed 13 Mar 2021
- 'Henri Winkelman', viewed 7 April 2021
- 'Herzogenbusch concentration camp', viewed 24 Mar 2021
- 'Het Parool', viewed 31 Mar, 2021
- 'History of the Jews in the Netherlands', viewed 16 Jul 2021
- Rudolph Cleveringa, viewed 21 May 2021
- 'Underground media in the German-occupied Netherlands, viewed 21 Jan 2022
- 'V-weapons', viewed 12 May 2021
- 'Walraven van Hall', viewed 21 May 2021
- 'Westerbork transit camp', viewed 24 Mar 2021
- 'Zone Libre', viewed 6 May 2021.

Wikipedia articles (Dutch edition): nl.wikipedia.org/wiki
- 'Van Ketwich', viewed 13 Apr 2021
- 'Henri Koot', viewed 1 Feb 2022
- 'Carel Kranenburg', viewed 30 Apr 2021
- 'Jean Mesritz', viewed 17 Jan 2022
- 'Kamp Rhede-Brual', viewed 21 Apr 2021
- 'Landelijke Organisatie voor Hulp aan Onderduikers', viewed 27 Jan 2021
- 'Lodo van Hamel', viewed 17 Jan 2021
- 'Netherlands in World War II', viewed 16 Jul 2021

- 'Trouw (verzetsblad)', viewed 31 Mar 2021
- 'Verzetskruis', viewed 17 Jan 2022.

private letters and other unpublished works

Asscher, Jacob Jr. 'Letter to Mrs Furstner' dated 13th September 1944. Translated by Dini Elting.

Béliard, Luc. 'Denis Mesritz: a brief summary' and 'From Leiden to England'. Unpublished research notes.

Furstner, Roosje. 'Notebook' from which we have some diary-style entries from April 1931 to June 1932, translated by Ron van Hasselt, courtesy of Ferdinand van Lelyveld.

van Ketwich Verschuur, Henricus. 'Letter to Monsieur Feuilletau de Bruyn', the Hague, dated 25 Feb 1945 & 27th July 1945. Translated by Dini Elting.

Mesritz, Denis, 'Letter to Charles Béliard', dated 27th November 1940. Translated by Dini Elting.

Mesritz, Léo. Unpublished diary, 1940.

Mesritz-Mulder, Maria Emelia Theresia. 'Letter to Claire Béliard', dated 15th November 1939. Translated by Dini Elting.

Michielsen, Karel. *Bygone Glory*. Unpublished memoirs, courtesy of Karel Michielsen Junior, 2013.

de Vos, Jacob. 'Letter to Léo Mesritz' from the Hague, dated 25 Jun 1945. Translated by Dini Elting.

Image Credits

Images not listed here are original photographs held or taken by members of the family.

Back cover: Robert Prummel at Dutch Wikipedia, CC BY-SA 3.0, commons.wikimedia.org/wiki/File:VERZETSKRUIS_1945.jpg

Figure 1: Margaret Marshall.

Figure 3: Courtesy of Megan Burrows.

Figure 4: Courtesy of Megan Burrows.

Figure 9: Compiled by Francis Bond.

Figure 16: Public domain from www.walravenfoundation.org/walravenvanhall.

Figure 17: Professor Telders (left) public domain from commons.wikimedia.org/wiki/File:BTelders.jpg and Professor Cleveringa (right) Courtesy of NIOD beeldbankwo2.nl/en/imagebank/detail/cf388358-0259-11e7-904b-d89d6717b464/media/364bd606-c54d-a349-3d7a-b16381c70a21.

Figure 20: Karel Michielsen (left) courtesy of Karel Michielsen Junior and Erik Michielsen (right) aircrewremembered.com/editorial/resources/michielsen-jfk-w800-w800.jpg.

Figure 22: Erik Hazelhoff, *Soldier of Orange.*

Figure 23: Public domain from www.75jaarvrijheid.nl/ artikel/2141392/lodo-van-hamel-spion-van-oranje

Figure 24: Public domain from commons.wikimedia.org/wiki/ File:Flickr_-_Erfgoed_in_Beeld_-_Visit_of_Queen_Wilhelmina_ and_Princess_Juliana_to_the_city_of_Breda.jpg (cropped).

Figure 25: Photo-typeset by Nicole Murray.

Figure 26: [Lodo van Hamel death notice], *De Telegraaf* [newspaper], 21 Jun 1941. p. 9. https://www.delpher.nl/nl/ kranten, viewed 21 May 2021

Figure 28: Public domain from www.deathcamps.org/ reinhard/pic/bigvughtmap.jpg.

Figure 30: Public domain from commons.wikimedia.org/wiki/ File:Willem_Karel_Hendrik_Feuilletau_de_Bruyn_(1886-1972). jpg.

Figure 31: Vitavia, CC BY-SA 4.0 commons.wikimedia.org/ wiki/File:Niederländisches_Ehrenfeld_FriedhofOhlsdorf_(2).jpg (converted to black and white).

Figure 37: Han Gelder (left) public domain from www.geni. com/photo/view/6000000069061019833?album_type=photos_ of_me&photo_id=6000000069061024821 and Wim Eggink (right) public domain from oorlogsgravenstichting.nl/persoon/38416/ willem-eggink.

Figure 38: Public domain from commons.wikimedia.org/w/ index.php?curid=37069276

Figure 39: Public domain from *Oranjehotel Book of the Dead* www.nationaalarchief.nl/onderzoeken/archief/2.19.136/invnr/3/file/NL-HaNA_2.19.136_3_0122-00002000003_121.

Figure 41: Newspaper clipping (left) [Denis Mesritz reburial], *Het Parool* [newspaper], 29 Mar 1949. p. 1. https://www.delpher.nl/nl/kranten, viewed 21 May 2021.

Figure 42: [Jean and Denis Mesritz death notice], *Het Parool* [newspaper], 17 Jul 1945. p. 2. https://www.delpher.nl/nl/kranten, viewed 21 May 2021..

Figure 45: Door Medalmaniak – Eigen werk, CC BY-SA 4.0, https://commons.wikimedia.org/w/index.php?curid=46557619

Figure 47: Courtesy of Ann Blake.

Figure 48: www.erelijst.nl/jean-adrien-claire--mesritz (upper) and www.erelijst.nl/denis-claire-baudouin--mesritz (lower)